ASEAN
Life After the Charter

**ASEAN
Studies Centre**
Institute of Southeast Asian Studies

The **ASEAN Studies Centre** of the Institute of Southeast Asian Studies in Singapore is devoted to working on issues that pertain to the Association of Southeast Asian Nations as an institution and a process, as distinct from the broader concerns of the Institute with respect to Southeast Asia.

Through research, conferences, consultations, and publications, the Centre seeks to illuminate ways of promoting ASEAN's purposes — political solidarity, economic integration and regional cooperation — and the obstacles on the path to achieving them. Through its studies, the Centre offers a measure of intellectual support to the ASEAN member-countries and the ASEAN Secretariat in building the ASEAN Community, with its political/security, economic and socio-cultural pillars. The Centre aims to conduct studies and make policy recommendations on issues and events that call for collective ASEAN actions and responses.

The Centre seeks to work together with other intellectual centres, institutes, think-tanks, foundations, universities, international and regional organizations, government agencies, and non-governmental organizations that have similar interests and objectives, as well as with individual scholars and the ASEAN Secretariat.

The **Institute of Southeast Asian Studies (ISEAS)** was established as an autonomous organization in 1968. It is a regional centre dedicated to the study of socio-political, security and economic trends and developments in Southeast Asia and its wider geostrategic and economic environment. The Institute's research programmes are the Regional Economic Studies (RES, including ASEAN and APEC), Regional Strategic and Political Studies (RSPS), and Regional Social and Cultural Studies (RSCS).

ISEAS Publishing, an established academic press, has issued more than 2,000 books and journals. It is the largest scholarly publisher of research about Southeast Asia from within the region. ISEAS Publishing works with many other academic and trade publishers and distributors to disseminate important research and analyses from and about Southeast Asia to the rest of the world.

ASEAN
Life After the Charter

Edited by **S. Tiwari**

LSEAS

INSTITUTE OF SOUTHEAST ASIAN STUDIES
Singapore

First published in Singapore in 2010 by
ISEAS Publishing
Institute of Southeast Asian Studies
30 Heng Mui Keng Terrace
Pasir Panjang
Singapore 119614
E-mail: publish@iseas.edu.sg
Website: http://bookshop.iseas.edu.sg

The responsibility for facts and opinions in this publication rests exclusively with the authors and their interpretations do not necessarily reflect the views or the policy of the Institute or its supporters.

ISEAS Library Cataloguing-in-Publication Data

ASEAN : life after the Charter / edited by S. Tiwari.
   1.   ASEAN.
   2.   ASEAN. Charter (2005)
   3.   Southeast Asia — Economic integration.
   4.   Southeast Asia — Economic policy.
   5.   Southeast Asia — Commercial policy.
   I.   Tiwari, S.
JZ5333.5 A9A844   2010

ISBN 978-981-4279-56-7 (hard cover)
ISBN 978-981-4279-55-0 (E-Book PDF)

Typeset by Superskill Graphics Pte Ltd
Printed in Singapore by Utopia Press Pte Ltd

CONTENTS

FOREWORD

ASEAN is at an exciting phase of its development. It has started to grapple with the meaning, implications and the implementation issues pertaining to the newly adopted ASEAN Charter. Concurrently, ASEAN is working intensively on integration-related economic issues for the creation of the ASEAN Economic Community by 2015. This is the first book which contains an in-depth analysis of aspects of the new ASEAN Charter and the trade in goods and the comprehensive investment agreements ASEAN has recently completed. The book deals with the key areas of legal personality conferred on ASEAN by the Charter; the legislation and other measures required by ASEAN member states to comply with the Charter; and the plan, progress and related issues relating to ASEAN's new trade in goods and comprehensive investment agreements. The book also highlights policy issues for consideration by ASEAN policy-makers. The book is edited by S. Tiwari, the former Head of the International Law Division in Singapore's Attorney-General's Chambers and currently a Visiting Senior Research Fellow at ISEAS. He was extensively involved in many aspects of ASEAN-related work, including negotiating and drafting of its key trade, investment and dispute settlement-related instruments.

Dr Surin Pitsuwan
Secretary-General of ASEAN

PREFACE

This is the first book which contains an in-depth analysis of aspects of the ASEAN Charter and its implementation, and the new goods and investment instruments that ASEAN has recently adopted. It is intended to start the process of creating a better understanding of the Charter and its implementation issues and the instruments underpinning the push towards economic integration and the ASEAN Economic Community.

A special feature of the book is the "Summary of Key Points" at the end of each chapter. I have prepared the summaries to enable readers to obtain an overview and a quick appreciation of each chapter.

I am indebted to Ambassador K. Kesavapany, Director of the Institute of Southeast Asian Studies (ISEAS) for his advice, guidance and encouragement in this book project. I am also grateful to the Head of the ASEAN Studies Centre at ISEAS, Mr Rodolfo Severino, who kindly read through the draft manuscript and offered useful suggestions.

I would like to thank all paper presenters and my colleagues, Mrs Y.L. Lee, Head of Administration, Ms Moe Thuzar, Ms Karthiani Nair, Mr Deepak Nair, Ms Emillia Amin and Mr Alex Tham Keng Sum. The workshop would not have been possible without support from them.

My special thanks to Mrs Triena Ong, Managing Editor of the ISEAS Publications Unit, who was always generous with her time in guiding me through the intricacies of preparing a book for publication. I also appreciate greatly the unstinting assistance of Ms Rahilah Yusof and Ms Sheryl Sin.

S. Tiwari
Editor
March 2010

LIST OF CONTRIBUTORS

Jeffrey Chan Wah Teck read law at the University of Singapore and Harvard University. He is currently the Deputy Solicitor-General. Previously he headed the Civil and then the International Affairs Division at the Singapore Attorney-General's Chambers. He was the first Chair of the High Level Legal Experts' Group (HLEG) on the follow-up to the ASEAN Charter and has since then been the HLEG member for Singapore.

Simon Chesterman is Global Professor and Director of the New York University (NYU) School of Law Singapore Programme, and a Professor of Law at the National University of Singapore. Prior to joining NYU, he was a Senior Associate at the International Peace Academy and Director of UN Relations at Crisis Group in New York. He has previously worked for the UN Office for the Coordination of Humanitarian Affairs in Yugoslavia and interned at the International Criminal Tribunal for Rwanda.

He has authored a number of books on the United Nations and on humanitarian intervention under international law.

Termsak Chalermpalanupap is currently Director of the Political and Security Directorate at the ASEAN Secretariat. He studied political science and has served at the Secretariat in various capacities since 1993, including as Special Assistant to the Secretary-General.

He has represented the ASEAN Secretariat in each of the groups working on the ASEAN Charter: the Eminent Persons Group, the High Level Task Force, the High Level Panel (drafting the Terms of Reference for the human rights body) and the High Level Legal Expert Group.

Michael Ewing-Chow is an Associate Professor at the National University of Singapore (NUS) where he teaches world trade law and corporate law. He received an LL.B. (First Class) from NUS and an LL.M. from Harvard.

Along with some colleagues, he started the first World Trade Law course at NUS. He has been a consultant to the Singapore Government as well as the World Bank and the WTO. He has written and published articles on trade law and investment law.

Kanya Satyani Sasradipoera is currently a Regional Cooperation Specialist at the Asian Development Bank. Prior to this appointment, she was the Senior Officer for Trade in Goods Unit at the ASEAN Secretariat. She obtained her Bachelor's Degree in Metallurgical Engineering from the University of Indonesia in 1994 and Master's Degree in Public Policy from the National University of Singapore in 2003.

She first joined the ASEAN Secretariat in 1996 as Assistant Programme Officer, then worked with the ASEAN-UNDP Sub-Regional Programme and rejoined the ASEAN Secretariat in 2004 as Special Officer. She commenced work with the Bureau for Economic Integration from 2005 as Senior Officer for Trade in Goods.

Yap Lai Peng holds a Bachelor of Economics and Masters of Public Administration from the University of Malaya. She also attended the Advanced Certificate on International Economics at the Kiel Institute of Economics in 1993/94. She started with the ASEAN Secretariat as a Trade Economist in October 2007 and then moved to her current position as Assistant Director, Head of Services and

Investment Division in November 2008. Prior to October 2007, she worked with the Malaysian Ministry of International Trade and Industry and the Malaysian Ministry of Finance.

Razeen Sally is Co-Director of the European Centre for International Political Economy (ECIPE), an international economic policy think-tank based in Brussels. He received his Ph.D. from the London School of Economics in 1992. He is a Senior Research Associate at the South African Institute of International Affairs in Johannesburg. He has been a Visiting Professor at the Institut D'Etudes Politiques (Sciences Po) in Paris, Visiting Senior Research Fellow at the Institute of Southeast Asian Studies in Singapore, a Visiting Fellow at the University of Hong Kong, and Director, Trade Policy, at the Commonwealth Business Council in London.

Eduardo Pedrosa is the Secretary-General of the Pacific Economic Cooperation Council (PECC), a position he has held since March 2006. He has worked on regional economic issues for fourteen years in various capacities. Before joining PECC in 2000 as Director of Policy, he was the Coordinator of the Regional Programme for Southeast Asia of the Konrad-Adenauer-Stiftung and was Co-Editor of its journal *Panorama*. He has also worked for the Economist Intelligence Unit. He is a graduate of the London School of Economics.

David Parsons is Executive Director of the Committee on Investment and International Trade Development in the Indonesian Chamber of Commerce and Industry — Kadin Indonesia. He joined the Chamber in 2005 to help develop more systematic policy contributions from the Indonesian business sector for the government's reform process.

Following earlier careers as a journalist, farmer and researcher at the Australian Bureau of Agricultural and Resource Economics, he joined PECC in 1988 and worked there till 2005 in various capacities.

Martin Hutagalung is the U.S.-ASEAN Business Council's Regional Director based in Singapore. Martin is the primary liaison point with Council members in the region and oversees the Council's programmes and services in Singapore. Before moving to Singapore, Martin was based in the Council's Washington D.C. office as Manager for ASEAN and APEC Affairs.

Martin holds an M.B.A. with a concentration in Management of Global Information Technology from the American University and received his B.B.A. with a concentration in International Business from the George Washington University.

Sivakant Tiwari is currently a Visiting Senior Research Fellow at the Institute of Southeast Asian Studies (ISEAS), Singapore, dealing with ASEAN-related Legal Affairs. Prior to joining ISEAS, he served in senior positions in the Singapore Legal Service.

During his stint in the Legal Service, Tiwari played a significant role in preparing the legislation for the newly formed Singapore Armed Forces. He led the evidence in landmark Commissions of Inquiry, represented Singapore in high profile internal security cases in the Singapore High Court and has led numerous bilateral and multilateral trade, investment, intellectual property, maritime boundary, law of the sea and other negotiations on behalf of Singapore. He has also been extensively involved in many aspects of ASEAN-related legal work, including negotiating, advising and drafting of its key trade, investment and dispute-related instruments. Tiwari was involved in handling Singapore's Pedra Branca case from the commencement of the dispute in 1979 till the hearing of the case at the International Court of Justice in November 2007. He served as a Panel Member (2007–08) in a major WTO intellectual property case involving the U.S. and China and is currently a Panel Member in the Tuna-II dispute at the WTO involving the U.S. and Mexico. He has contributed articles, *inter alia*, on trade and intellectual property issues.

INTRODUCTION

BACKGROUND

The Association of Southeast Asian Nations (ASEAN) was established on 8 August 1967 in Bangkok by the ASEAN Declaration. ASEAN had only five members at the time of its establishment: Indonesia, Malaysia, Philippines, Singapore and Thailand. The ASEAN Declaration spelt out the aspirations of the five nations and indicated a simple informal structure to carry them out.

Over the years, ASEAN expanded into a ten-member body with the following additional members: Brunei, Vietnam, Laos, Myanmar and Cambodia. Forty years on, it also finds itself in a very different globalized world of intense economic competition.

In adapting ASEAN to the changed environment, ASEAN leaders decided that ASEAN needed a meaningful instrument to spell out the aims, aspirations, vision, powers and structure of ASEAN. Hence, the ASEAN Charter was signed by the ASEAN states on 20 November 2007 at the 13th ASEAN Summit in Singapore. It entered into force on 15 December 2008, this date being the thirtieth day after all ten ASEAN member states had deposited their instruments of ratification with the Secretary-General of ASEAN.

What does the Charter do for ASEAN? In the words of the current ASEAN Secretary-General, Dr Surin Pitsuwan, the Charter:

... has helped ASEAN articulate our values, purposes, visions and foundations on which we are built and our desire to build a regional identity... It is now up to the stakeholders of ASEAN to take up the challenge of regional integration to respond creatively to globalisation and the opportunity to improve our lives. Although many challenges lie ahead, the ASEAN Charter gives us hope, purpose and importantly a framework of action for all the peoples of ASEAN.

(Extracted from the Foreword by the
ASEAN Secretary-General to the book,
The Making of the ASEAN Charter, edited by Tommy Koh,
Rosario G. Manalo and Walter Woon)

The ASEAN Charter, also referred to as the "little green book", is akin to a constitutional instrument for ASEAN. It will be studied, analysed, interpreted and written about for years to come. It will be applied on a daily basis. ASEAN political leaders, parliamentarians and government officials, ASEAN Secretariat officers, civil society members, and the public in general, all need to have at least a general understanding of what the Charter means.

EMERGING ISSUES

ASEAN is at the threshold of an exciting period. It has started to grapple with the meaning and implications of the Charter provisions and the issues pertaining to its implementation.

ASEAN is at the same time working intensively on economic issues. It has a strong economic potential with a combined market of almost 600 million people. To benefit from this potential, ASEAN needs to integrate and do so rapidly. It has thus accelerated the achievement of economic integration from 2020 to 2015.

With the objective of creating the necessary environment for the free movement of goods and a freer and more open investment regime, two legal instruments consolidating ASEAN agreements on trade and investments were reviewed and revised in 2009. These instruments are the ASEAN Trade in Goods Agreement 2009 (ATIGA) and the ASEAN Comprehensive Investment Agreement 2009 (ACIA). The follow-up work on these two instruments will have an important bearing on how ASEAN's economic integration objectives are accomplished.

COMPLEMENTING THE ASEAN PROCESS: WORKSHOP AND ISSUES TAKEN UP

(a) Issues ASEAN is Grappling with

To assist in the work relating to the Charter and economic issues, the ASEAN Studies Centre (ASC) at the Institute of Southeast Asian Studies (ISEAS) organized a workshop entitled, "Life After the Charter", on 27–28 July 2009, at ISEAS in Singapore. The workshop was intended to provide a forum to study, analyse and brainstorm the issues that ASEAN is grappling with currently. The workshop dealt with the following issues:

(i)   the nature, meaning and implications of the legal personality conferred by the Charter on ASEAN;
(ii) the legislation and other measures required by ASEAN member countries to implement the Charter; and
(iii) the plan, progress and connected issues in relation to the recently completed agreements on trade in goods and investment.

The workshop aimed to complement the ASEAN process by pooling together the insights of the practitioners, scholars, opinion-makers and business people with the experience and knowledge of government and ASEAN officials closely involved in the legal personality and implementation issues and the work on the two agreements. Views and perspectives from the business sector and those in academia knowledgeable on ASEAN issues and treaties enriched the discussions.

The workshop took up the legal personality of ASEAN as the first area for study, as it is a key component of the Charter. The implications of the issue need to be settled so that ASEAN countries can legislate on it and implement it. This would allow, *inter alia*, actions taken by ASEAN as an entity to have a legal basis.

(b) Summary of Presentations and Discussions

The chapters which follow also contain summaries of the key points of the presentations and the discussions. These have been prepared to provide a quick appreciation of the issues and thus make the publication more useful.

(c) Conclusions and Policy Issues

The conclusions and policy issues arising from the workshop have been developed in a separate chapter for study and consideration by ASEAN countries.

I

ASEAN LEGAL PERSONALITY UNDER ITS NEW CHARTER — ITS NATURE, MEANING AND IMPLICATIONS
Status of the Work and Issues Involved

Jeffrey Chan Wah Teck

Legal personality is an attribute that is necessary in order for a person or entity to enter into legal relationships. Only legal persons can enjoy and enforce legal rights and obligations. In all national jurisdictions, whether or not a person or an entity is a legal person is determined by the domestic law of that jurisdiction. Internationally, this is determined by the rules of Public International Law. Legal personality of an entity is manifested in its capacity to sue or be sued in domestic or international courts and tribunals.

LEGAL PERSONS

Under the domestic laws of all nations, a legal person can either be a natural person, that is, an individual human being, or an artificial person. For a natural person, legal personality attaches at birth. Until birth, a person does not possess legal personality and thus cannot sue or be sued for matters occurring prior to his or her birth.

Artificial persons in domestic law are entities that are incorporated under domestic laws and conferred legal personality by law upon incorporation. Incorporation can be by registration, as in the case of companies. Alternatively, incorporation can be by statutes passed by Parliament. For example, in Singapore, statutory boards are all established by legislation which confers the body with legal personality and provides that it can sue and be sued. Historically, in some states, entities can also be incorporated by writs issued by the sovereign. Examples of these would be the many trading bodies during the heyday of European colonial expansion such as the Chartered Bank and the East India Company.

An artificial person is separate from a natural person or the entity involved in it. This means that the rights and liabilities of an artificial person are distinct from those of the natural person and entities, whether incorporated or not, who are its constituents.

INTERNATIONAL LEGAL PERSON

All states are international legal persons and possess international legal personality. But they would achieve this standing only if they satisfy the attributes of statehood recognized by Public International Law. States can be members of international organizations, which can also include regional organizations. International organizations can also include international entities other than states, for example, non-governmental organizations and national liberation movements. Whatever may be its constituent members, an international organization would be an international legal person only when it is recognized as possessing legal personality under Public International Law. This does not depend on whether or not that international organization declares itself to be a legal person. It is determined largely by the actions of that international organization, whether what it does requires it to have legal personality, and the reactions of other international actors with whom it relates. Thus, if an international organization acts as if it is a legal person, such as entering into legal relationships with other international actors, and if those with whom it relates recognizes it as possessing legal personality, it can safely be concluded that that organization does enjoy international legal personality, even if it does not declare itself to be such.

Like legal persons in domestic jurisdictions, an international organization with legal personality is a legal person that is separate from the states and/or other entities that can constitute it. An international legal person would be able to enjoy rights and also incur liabilities under public international law. It can enter into treaties and initiate or defend proceedings before international tribunals, such as the International Court of Justice. In domestic jurisdictions, it can enjoy the same capacities as domestic legal persons. However, it can enjoy such capacities only if it is recognized by the domestic law of that jurisdiction as possessing legal personality.

ASEAN

ASEAN is an organization of the states of Southeast Asia. It was established by treaty and governed by agreements reached between its constituent member states. Initially, ASEAN operated on an informal and consensual basis. Thus no enforcement mechanisms were put in place to ensure compliance with the many agreements reached among ASEAN member states. This changed significantly when the ASEAN Charter came into effect in 2008.

The ASEAN Charter is the result of recognition by the member states of ASEAN that ASEAN has matured to a point where it is ready for a higher level of not just economic but also social and political integration. The Charter is based on recommendations made by an Eminent Persons Group which comprised the elder statesmen of ASEAN. It was drafted by a High Level Task Force and adopted in Singapore in November 2007. It has been ratified by all ASEAN member states and came into force in 2008.

The main purpose of the ASEAN Charter was to establish ASEAN as a rules-based organization. To this effect, the ASEAN Charter sets out numerous objectives, organizational structures and processes for ASEAN. Central to the ASEAN Charter and the main feature of ASEAN as a rules-based organization are the provisions on the settlement of disputes. These are set out in Chapter VIII of the Charter. These provisions are designed to ensure that disputes among ASEAN member states on interpretations and applications of the ASEAN Charter are settled through processes that ensure that such agreements are given full effect. This would ensure that the conduct and affairs of ASEAN are compliant with the rule of law.

The central features of any regime based on the Rule of Law are as follows:

- The outcomes of actions are governed by clear, transparent and accessible rules;
- Such outcomes are enforceable, whether through penalties, sanctions or moral suasion;
- Arbitrariness in the exercise of power and uncertainty of outcomes are minimized.

Fundamental to the Rule of Law and a rules-based organization are mechanisms for accountability and agreed rules that are applicable to all.

For an organization to be rules-based, it must first be clothed with legal personality. Without legal personality, it will not be able to apply or enforce its rules as well as rules which either it binds itself, or bind others to. The organization must also be subject to a strong dispute resolution mechanism. This would ensure that any party who attempts to repudiate an obligation that it has bound itself to can be brought to an independent authority and declared to be in the wrong. This same consideration applies to the need for an enforcement mechanism as without such mechanisms, obligations agreed to can be treated with impunity. As mentioned previously, an enforcement mechanism can be in the form of penalties, sanctions or moral suasion.

THE ASEAN CHARTER

Article 3 of the ASEAN Charter proclaims as follows:

> "ASEAN, as an inter-governmental organization, is hereby conferred legal personality."

Article 25 of the ASEAN Charter then proceeds to provide for a Dispute Settlement Mechanism ("DSM") in the following terms:

> "Where not otherwise specifically provided, appropriate dispute resolution mechanisms, including arbitration, shall be established for disputes which concern the interpretation or application of this Charter and other ASEAN instruments."

The ASEAN Charter has put in place principles and directions for ASEAN and its institutions. To operationalize the Charter, rules and processes are needed to be put in place. In this regard, ASEAN established two working groups to give effect to the ASEAN Charter. These are the High Level Panel (HLP) which was to operationalize the provisions of the Charter relating to the ASEAN Human Rights Mechanism and the High Level Experts' Group (HLEG). The HLEG was appointed in July 2007 and comprises senior legal experts from all ten ASEAN countries. They are legally qualified senior diplomats or senior government legal advisers. These experts are assisted by a team of assistants, most of whom are legally qualified, and are provided with administrative support by the ASEAN Secretariat (ASEC). Senior officials of the ASEC also assisted the HLEG as resource persons on the practices of ASEAN as an institution.

The terms of reference of the HLEG, as provided by the ASEAN Foreign Ministers, required the HLEG to address the following areas in the ASEAN Charter:

(a) Legal personality of ASEAN in accordance with Article 3 of the ASEAN Charter;
(b) Dispute Settlement Mechanism in accordance with Articles 25 and 26; and
(c) Other legal issues under the ASEAN Charter.

The chair of the HLEG followed the chair of ASEAN. Initially Singapore held the chair but this was rotated to Thailand when the ASEAN chair was rotated to Thailand. HLEG has, up to July 2009, held fourteen meetings. These were held in rotation among all the ASEAN member states and in the premises of the ASEC in Jakarta. The draft texts and materials for discussions were prepared by Thailand while individual members were each assigned to prepare texts on specific issues being considered by HLEG. Singapore was assigned to prepare the draft rules on how persons are to be authorized to sign domestic and international agreements on behalf of ASEAN. In addition, when necessary, individual HLEG members would table non-papers to set out their position on specific issues under discussion. A Summary Record was produced at the end of each meeting by ASEC officers. This was then vetted by the HLEG assistants and confirmed by HLEG through consensus. The Summary Records constitute the *travaux preparatoires* of the texts produced by the HLEG. All HLEG discussions were held in plenary and all issues were discussed and concluded through open discussion. All decisions were reached through consensus in the same way as most decisions of ASEAN.

At the outset, the HLEG identified that it needed to undertake work on the following instruments:

(1) An agreement on the privileges and immunities of ASEAN in order to give effect to the legal personality of ASEAN and also

to provide privileges and immunities to the ASEC; Permanent Representatives of ASEAN member states to ASEAN; officials on ASEAN missions; experts and officials of member states. This agreement, when in force, would ensure that as a legal person, ASEAN will enjoy the same legal capacities in all ASEAN member states. Additionally, officials contemplated in this agreement will be conferred with the same privileges and immunities and at the same level in all ASEAN member states when they are carrying out activities on behalf of ASEAN.

(2) The ASEAN Dispute Settlement Protocol, which will be a protocol to the ASEAN Charter and would set out the various processes for the settlement of disputes over the interpretation and application of the ASEAN Charter and other ASEAN instruments. Such processes include conciliation, mediation and arbitration. As the Charter provides that unresolved disputes are to be referred to the ASEAN Summit, it was agreed that this Protocol will also include rules as to what constitutes an unresolved dispute within the contemplation of the Charter, and the processes to be observed when referring this to the ASEAN Summit.

(3) In addition, the HLEG also decided to work on a range of subsidiary instruments, including rules to prescribe who are authorized to bind ASEAN in transactions under domestic law and under international law.

PROGRESS OF HLEG

HLEG has completed the Agreement on the Privileges and Immunities of ASEAN. It has also almost completed the text of the *"Authorizations for Entering into Transactions in Domestic Law on behalf of ASEAN"*, and has made substantial initial progress in its deliberations on *"Authorizations for Signature of International Agreements on behalf of ASEAN"*. Discussion on the other draft texts, including the DSM Protocol under Article 25 of the ASEAN Charter, are still in progress. However, the progress of HLEG has been slow. This was due to some extent to the very diverse laws and legal systems in ASEAN which require all the participants in the discussion to make substantial efforts to understand each other's position before being able to deliberate the issues in contention effectively. There were also differences in the understandings amongst various HLEG members of the underlying premises of the ASEAN Charter.

ASEAN LEGAL PERSONALITY

The fact that Article 3 of the ASEAN Charter declares ASEAN to be established as a legal person manifests an understanding on the part of ASEAN that until the Charter came about, ASEAN, as an institution, had no legal personality. This understanding was borne out by ASEAN practices to date. All binding international agreements between ASEAN and other states or organizations are entered into between the other party or parties and all the member states of ASEAN, and not by ASEAN as a single legal person. There are, however, a range of non-binding instruments, often loosely termed as Memorandums of Understanding (MOU), which were signed by one or more persons on behalf of ASEAN. Such instruments do not evince intentions to create legal relations and thus the issue whether ASEAN was a legal person did not arise.

Although ASEAN may not be a legal person prior to the Charter, its Secretariat viz., "ASEC" has operated in many jurisdictions, notably in Indonesia where it has its headquarters, as a legal person. ASEC was incorporated under Indonesian domestic law as a legal person and thus can enter into legal transactions in Indonesia. It has in fact entered into a substantial number of legal transactions since its inception. These include the purchase of goods and services and employment of officials and staff. ASEC may well have operated as a legal person in other domestic jurisdictions and entered into legal transactions there, even though it was not established as a legal person in those jurisdictions. In so doing, ASEC would have relied on its legal personality under Indonesian law.

It is somewhat questionable that the ASEC was a legal person, when the parent entity, that is, ASEAN, was not.

AGREEMENT ON THE PRIVILEGES AND IMMUNITIES OF ASEAN (ASEAN P & I AGREEMENT)

The structure of this agreement which HLEG completed was based on the 1946 Convention on the Privileges and Immunities of the United Nations (UNCPI). Like the UNCPI, the ASEAN P & I Agreement declares that ASEAN is an international legal person and thus able to act as such. It has the capacity to enter into and enforce binding international legal obligations. The main purpose of providing for this in an ASEAN agreement was to ensure that the legal capacities of ASEAN are harmonized such that ASEAN would have the same legal status and capacities in all its member states and any other state that would be a party to this agreement. This ensures legal certainty for ASEAN as well as for all parties dealing with ASEAN and is an important factor for a rules-based organization.

The critical aspect of legal personality is how ASEAN as a legal person can go about acting as such. Article 2(1) of the ASEAN Charter provides that ASEAN shall have the following capacities under domestic laws:

(a) To enter into contracts;
(b) To acquire and dispose of moveable and immoveable properties; and
(c) To institute and defend itself in legal proceedings.

The article provides that in the exercise of these capacities, ASEAN shall be represented by the Secretary-General, the Deputy Secretaries-General and other officers of the ASEAN Secretariat authorized by the Secretary-General. On the international plane, the Charter provides that in exercising its capacities under international law, including the power of concluding agreements under Article 41(7) of the ASEAN Charter, ASEAN shall act through representatives authorized by its member states.

In order to operationalize this provision, HLEG is currently working on rules to set out how persons can be authorized to represent ASEAN in the exercise of its legal personality in domestic jurisdictions as well in the international sphere. These rules will be annexed to the ASEAN P & I Agreement and would enable parties dealing with ASEAN both in the domestic as well as international sphere to ascertain whether or not the person that they are dealing with is authorized to bind ASEAN . When enacted into domestic law, these rules will have the force of law in ASEAN member states as well as in all other states that agree to be a party to this agreement. As these rules set out various administrative processes for ASEC, including the requirement to make it publicly known who are the persons authorized to bind ASEAN in a legal transaction, they will also be in the nature of administrative instructions for the ASEC to comply with.

PRIVILEGES AND IMMUNITIES (P & I)

"Privileges and immunities" refer to exemptions granted to a person by a host or a receiving state from the operation of its domestic laws and regulations. This originated from diplomatic practice and was based on reciprocity amongst sovereigns. A sovereign would not subject another sovereign who was in his territory to the force of his own laws so long as the other sovereign would do the same. This rule, in the main, protected envoys sent by one sovereign to the territory of another. Envoys represent the person of his sovereign in the territory of the other sovereign. Being conferred with exemptions from the laws of the host or receiving sovereign means that should relations between the two sovereigns deteriorate, the host or receiving sovereign cannot use his laws to persecute that envoy. If he does so, then the other sovereign can do likewise with his envoy who is in the territory of that other sovereign.

The present law on diplomatic privileges and immunities is largely to be found in the 1969 Vienna Convention on the Law of Treaties and the 1986 Convention on the Law of Treaties between States and International Organizations or between International Organizations. The 1986 Convention has not yet entered into force. However, both these Conventions are often referred to, even by states who are not parties to them, as prescribing standards to be observed in the practice of privileges and immunities between states and between states and international organizations.

In recent times, it has become common for persons and entities to demand for privileges and immunities from states even though they are not envoys or representatives of international organizations. It is often asserted that they require exemption from the laws of the states where they operate in in order to assist that state or to carry out some objective that that state is bound to support. This is notwithstanding that other persons or organizations have effectively pursued similar objectives in the same jurisdiction without being conferred exemptions from its laws and regulations. The demand for privileges and immunities from a state may well be driven by the fact that obtaining exemptions from laws is a privileged status. Those with this status thus can hold themselves out as more distinguished and desirable than those who do not. For many organizations in the non-governmental sector who compete, often fiercely, with other non-governmental organizations pursuing similar objectives, this can be a major factor in attracting funding. Obtaining exemptions from national laws also, as should be obvious, contributes substantially to the recipient's sense of self-worth.

Apart from this, compelling a state to grant exemptions from its laws to nationals or agents of another state is a manifestation of the latter's power. This can be seen in the demands for extra-territoriality in the "unequal treaties" imposed on nineteenth-century China by the Western powers. Nineteenth-century China was a weak state and compelling it to exempt nationals of the Western powers from its laws was a pointed constant reminder to China by the Western powers where its place was in the international order. The present manifestation of this are the various non-reciprocal Status of Forces Agreements where powerful states obtain for their military servicemen immunity from the laws of weaker states where their military servicemen are present.

At the present time, agreements conferring privileges and immunites on national or agents of other states and on international organizations are very rarely based on reciprocity, which was the original basis for the grant of privileges and immunities. Privileges and immunities are conferred often without sensitivity to the fact these are in fact exemptions granted to foreigners from the laws of the state where they are in. The cost of granting such exemptions falls not on the government of the state that granted these, but on the people of that state. Granting exemptions from criminal laws expose the common folk of that jurisdiction to criminal actions which are neither deterred nor can be punished. Exemption from the civil laws of that jurisdiction exposes its people to losses for which they have no recourse to legal remedies.

PRIVILEGES AND IMMUNITIES OF ASEAN

ASEAN is not a sovereign and thus would not enjoy immunities in the domestic jurisdictions of other states. This is unless the domestic laws of all states where ASEAN may be present provide for immunities for ASEAN. These domestic laws must also provide for the limits of the capacities that ASEAN is to enjoy. If ASEAN is to enjoy privileges and immunities in domestic jurisdictions, then the persons who carry out the functions of ASEAN must be conferred with privileges and immunities. As a legal person, ASEAN can only act through natural persons. The immunities that ASEAN may enjoy in a domestic jurisdiction would be illusory unless the persons through whom ASEAN acts are also conferred privileges and immunities in that jurisdiction.

As such, the ASEAN P & I Agreement also provides for the privileges and immunities of persons who undertake the activities of ASEAN. These would be natural persons such as the Secretary-General, Deputy Secretaries-General and other officials of ASEAN; as well as Permanent Representatives of member states of ASEAN, their officers and staff, and officials of member countries who are engaged in ASEAN activities. All these categories of persons are referred to in the ASEAN Charter but as there can be different understandings of which persons would fall within each or any of these categories, the agreement carefully defines who these persons are, and also the extent of privileges and immunities that they would enjoy in the domestic jurisdictions of the states parties to the agreement.

The privileges and immunities set out in the ASEAN P & I Agreement would be effective only in the domestic jurisdictions of states who are parties to this agreement. While it is intended that all ASEAN member states would be parties to this agreement, for ASEAN to be able to operate fully and effectively as an international legal person and a regional organization, it would be imperative for ASEAN to enjoy privileges and immunities in other states as well, particularly in those states where ASEAN would have a presence. This can come about if these states are also parties to the ASEAN P & I Agreement. There is, therefore a need to inform other states of this agreement and to encourage them to sign on as parties.

STATUS OF WORK

The Agreement on the Privileges and Immunities of ASEAN as completed by HLEG has been submitted to and was accepted by the ASEAN Foreign Ministers at the 42nd ASEAN Ministerial Meeting held in Phuket in July 2009. HLEG has suggested that this agreement be signed by ASEAN Foreign Ministers at the ASEAN Summit to be held at Phuket in October 2009. It has urged all ASEAN member states to ratify this agreement expeditiously and to ensure that the necessary laws are enacted to give legal effect to this agreement in their respective domestic jurisdictions. The agreement will enter into force only upon ratification by all the member states of ASEAN. This may take some time.

The completion of this Agreement was an important achievement for HLEG. HLEG is continuing with its work on the other documents which it had identified that it needed to work on to give legal effect to the ASEAN Charter and to the ASEAN P & I Agreement. The most important document in this regard is the Dispute Settlement Protocol under Article 25 of the Charter and its accompanying rules on conciliation, mediation and arbitration. HLEG will in addition be working on the rules for the reference of unresolved disputes to the ASEAN Summit as contemplated by Article 26 of the ASEAN Charter.

The ASEAN Foreign Ministers have at the 42nd ASEAN Ministerial Meeting set a time limit for the HLEG to complete its work. HLEG may complete its work by the ASEAN Summit in October 2009. HLEG therefore will have to redouble its efforts and improve the speed and efficiency of its processes if this target date is to be met.

SUMMARY OF KEY POINTS

S. Tiwari

(a) The Nature of Legal Personality

Legal personality is necessary for legal relationships and for enjoying and enforcing legal rights and obligations. Within national jurisdictions, legal personality is determined by the rules of national law. Internationally, it is determined by the rules of Public International Law. Thus an international organization would be treated as an international legal person only when it is recognized as possessing a legal personality under Public International Law.

An international organization with legal personality is a legal entity which is separate from the states that are members of the organization. It may, in accordance with the terms of its constituent instrument, enter into treaties and initiate and defend proceedings in international tribunals and enjoy other rights under international law. It can enjoy the same capacities as domestic legal persons if it is recognized as possessing legal personality under domestic law.

The ASEAN Charter is the result of a recognition by the member states of ASEAN that ASEAN has matured to a point where it is ready for a higher level of not just economic but also political integration. Based on the recommendations of an Eminent Persons Group of elder statesmen of ASEAN and drafted by a High Level Task Force of senior government representatives, the Charter has been ratified by all ASEAN member states and came into force on 15 December 2008.

(b) Legal Capacity of the ASEAN Secretariat prior to the Charter

Although ASEAN may not have been a legal person prior to the Charter, the ASEAN Secretariat (ASEC) operated in Indonesia — where it has its headquarters — as a legal person. On 20 January 1979, the ASEC entered into the Agreement between the Government of Indonesia and ASEAN Relating to the Privileges and Immunities of the ASEAN Secretariat. This agreement provides, *inter alia*, that the Secretariat shall have the capacity (within Indonesia) to conclude contracts, to acquire and dispose of immoveable and moveable properties and to institute legal proceedings. Based on this arrangement, ASEC has been able to deal with the purchase of goods and services and employment of officials and staff in Indonesia.

(c) The Planned Work

The ASEAN Charter has put in place principles, rules, procedures and directions for ASEAN and its institutions. These need to be operationalized. Accordingly, a High Level Experts Group (HLEG) was appointed and tasked to address the areas of legal personality, dispute settlement mechanism and other legal issues under the ASEAN Charter.

In order to give effect to the legal personality of ASEAN and to provide privileges and immunities:

(i)   for ASEAN, which are necessary for the fulfilment of its purposes in the territory of member states;

(ii) for the Secretary-General of ASEAN and the staff of the ASEAN Secretariat participating in official ASEAN activities or representing ASEAN in member states, as are necessary for the independent exercise of their functions;

(iii) for the Permanent Representatives of ASEAN member states to ASEAN and officials of the member states participating in official ASEAN activities or representing ASEAN in member states, as are necessary for the exercise of their functions.

HLEG completed an agreement to prescribe privileges and immunities for ASEAN. This agreement, when completed and in force, would ensure that, as a legal person, ASEAN will enjoy the same legal capacities in all ASEAN member states. Additionally, officials contemplated in this agreement will be conferred with the same privileges and immunities and at the same level in all ASEAN member states when they are engaged in ASEAN activities.

(d) ASEAN Dispute Settlement Mechanism

HLEG is in the process of completing the ASEAN Dispute Settlement Protocol, which will be a Protocol to the ASEAN Charter. This would set out the various processes for the settlement of disputes over the interpretation or application of the ASEAN Charter and other ASEAN instruments. These processes include conciliation, mediation and arbitration. As the Charter provides that unresolved disputes are to be referred to the ASEAN Summit, this protocol will also include rules as to what constitutes an unresolved dispute within the contemplation of the Charter, and the processes to be observed when referring unresolved disputes to the ASEAN Summit.

(e) Other Subsidiary Instruments

The HLEG is also looking into a range of subsidiary instruments, including rules to prescribe who are authorized to bind ASEAN in transactions under domestic law and under international law.

(f) Progress of Work up to July 2009

The HLEG has completed the Agreement on the Privileges and Immunities of ASEAN (ASEAN P & I Agreement). It has also mostly completed the text of the "Authorisations for entering into transactions in Domestic Law on behalf of ASEAN" and has made progress in its deliberations on "Authorisations for Signature of International Agreements on behalf of ASEAN". Discussions on the other draft texts, including the ASEAN Dispute Settlement Mechanism Protocol, are still ongoing. Progress has been slow due to the diverse legal systems in ASEAN and differences in the understanding of HLEG members as to the underlying premises of the ASEAN Charter.

2

DOES ASEAN EXIST?
The Association of Southeast Asian Nations as an International Legal Person

Simon Chesterman

The ASEAN Charter, which entered into force on 15 December 2008, asserts in Article 3 that ASEAN "as an inter-governmental organisation, is hereby conferred legal personality". This chapter examines the legal status of the Association, as well as the political question of whether the whole is greater than (or perhaps less than) the sum of its parts. The argument presented is that legal personality at the international level is less a status than it is a capacity: the fact that ASEAN now claims international legal personality in the Charter does not mean it lacked it previously, nor that it now possesses it in any meaningful way. Rather, the key question is what specific powers have been granted to ASEAN and how those powers are used. On these questions, the Charter is largely silent.

* * *

In January 1991, less than two weeks before the commencement of hostilities to drive Iraq from occupied Kuwait, the French post-structuralist philosopher Jean Baudrillard published an article in *Libération* entitled, "The Gulf War Will Not Take Place". He argued that this war would never happen in a meaningful sense of the word, because technology had transformed perceptions of conflict to the point where all that was left was the simulacrum of war. As the bombs were falling and troops were moving, he produced a follow-up piece: "The Gulf War Is Not Taking Place". After Iraq had been driven from Kuwait and tens of thousands had died, he returned to the opinion pages with "The Gulf War Did Not Take Place". The three essays are now conveniently published together in a volume by Polity Press entitled *The Gulf War Never Happened.*[1]

Is it not a similar conceit to question the existence of ASEAN? Without doubt, the Association of Southeast Asian Nations (ASEAN) represents an important slice of the world. It encompasses a population of around half a billion, with a combined GDP in the order of a trillion U.S. dollars. From the five countries that signed the Bangkok Declaration in 1967,[2] it has added Brunei in 1984, and Vietnam, Laos, Myanmar, and Cambodia between 1995 and 1999.

But the key questions raised in this chapter are, first, what exactly is ASEAN in international legal terms? Secondly, whether in political terms ASEAN is greater than the sum of its parts: in other words, whether ASEAN as an entity offers something more than the ten separate nation states that constitute it. We can think of these questions as, first, does ASEAN exist? And, secondly, does ASEAN matter?

I. DOES ASEAN EXIST?

What *is* ASEAN? In particular, what is its legal status? Clearly it is more than just a "group of friends", ten states that share some limited set of interests and goals;[3] but clearly it is also less than the United Nations (UN), an international organization that asserts the power to impose binding obligations on all states.[4] It is more than an annual meeting of foreign ministers hoping to promote economic growth, but less than the World Trade Organization. Of the world's significant regional organizations, the powers ceded by members to the centre are less than within the European Union (EU), the African Union (AU), or the Organization of American States (OAS). Yet within Asia, it is perhaps the most important regional organization, with a wider mandate than the Asia-Pacific Economic Cooperation forum (APEC) and deeper commitments than the Shanghai Cooperation Organization (SCO).

Speaking in 1998, in the wake of an economic crisis that shocked the region's "tigers" and "dragons", the Secretary-General of ASEAN, Rodolfo Severino, gave a speech in which he emphasized that ASEAN "is not and was not meant to be a supranational entity acting independently of its members. It has no regional parliament or council of ministers with law-making powers, no power of enforcement, no judicial system."[5] He later reaffirmed more bluntly that ASEAN lacks "juridical personality or legal standing under international law".[6] This was consistent with the view that ASEAN was intended to be a kind of social community, rather than a legal community.[7]

A decade later, ASEAN has a Charter stating that, "ASEAN, as an inter-governmental organisation, is hereby conferred legal personality."[8] On 15 December 2008, that Charter came into effect thirty days after the tenth instrument of ratification had been deposited with the ASEAN Secretary-General.[9]

Does this mean that ASEAN before that moment had no international legal personality? And that after the entry into force of the Charter such personality miraculously popped into existence? The answer to both questions is a qualified "no": the lack of such a provision did not mean that ASEAN lacked international legal personality; the presence of one does not mean that it possesses personality in a meaningful sense. This section will briefly outline the basis of a test for international legal personality before applying it to ASEAN.

International Legal Personality

In every legal system, certain entities are regarded as possessing rights and duties enforceable at law. The recognition of those entities as "legal persons" is itself determined by law, a tautology that is reinforced in international law by the centrality of states not merely to the form, but also to the substance of its norms.[10] The practice and consent of states remain axiomatic to the concept of international law, and through the protection of territorial integrity and sovereign immunity, states are its primary beneficiaries.[11] This is replicated in the institutions of international order: only states are recognized as members of the UN; only states may bring contentious claims before the International Court of Justice.[12] (This is distinct from the question of whether an entity's legal personality is recognized in the domestic law of a given state,[13] a point frequently confused in literature[14] and, occasionally, in treaties.[15])

Nevertheless, international organizations, most prominently the UN itself, and some other entities (the Knights of Malta, for example) have been recognized as having international legal personality. The issue came before the International Court of Justice soon after the creation of the UN when Count Bernadotte, a Swedish national and chief UN truce negotiator in the Middle East, was killed in Jerusalem. The question concerned whether the UN had the capacity to bring an action in its own right against Israel with respect to his death. The court issued an advisory opinion that the UN did indeed have a measure of legal personality, derived from the consent of the states that established it:

> the Organization was intended to exercise and enjoy, and is in fact exercising and enjoying, functions and rights which can only be explained on the basis of the possession of a large measure of international personality and the capacity to operate upon an international plane. It is at present the supreme type of international organization, and it could not carry out the intentions of its founders if it was devoid of international personality. It must be

acknowledged that its Members, by entrusting certain functions
to it, with the attendant duties and responsibilities, have clothed
it with the competence required to enable those functions to be
effectively discharged.[16]

A complication, however, was that Israel was not yet among those
members.[17] The court went on to hold, nonetheless, that "fifty States,
representing the vast majority of the members of the international
community, had the power, in conformity with international law,
to bring into being an entity possessing *objective* international
personality, and not merely personality recognized by them alone."[18]

Six decades later international legal scholars are still arguing
about the two theories that can be derived from this advisory
opinion.

I. Will Theory

The "will theory" is most widely accepted and corresponds to the
first leg of the court's opinion. If the founders of an international
organization intend to endow their creation with personality, then
that is what it will receive. This theory is supported by the
understanding of international law as being based on the freely
expressed consent of states.

In the case of the UN, legal personality was not explicitly
asserted, but today it frequently is. Many international organizations
assert international legal personality in their constitutive documents,
for example, the International Seabed Authority,[19] the International
Criminal Court,[20] and the International Olive Oil Council.[21] The
Shanghai Cooperation Organization provides in its Charter that:

> As a subject of international law, SCO shall have international
> legal capacity… SCO shall enjoy the rights of a legal person and
> may in particular: conclude treaties; acquire movable and
> immovable property and dispose of it; appear in court as litigant;
> open accounts and have monetary transactions made.[22]

When its Charter entered into force, ASEAN joined such bodies.

Interestingly, some of the major regional organizations are not among this group. The EU's failed Constitution would have provided clearly that it enjoys legal personality. In its absence, the European Community certainly does have legal personality, but the EU itself is more ambiguous, having limited powers to enter into treaties only.[23] This would have changed if the Treaty of Lisbon had been ratified, as it proposed to add to the Treaty on European Union a provision that, "The Union shall have legal personality."[24] The Constitutive Act of the African Union does not provide explicitly for its legal personality, possibly on the assumption that it would inherit that of the Organization of African Unity.[25] The Organization of American States does not provide for its own legal personality.[26]

As indicated in the *Reparations* case, however, the failure specifically to outline the intention to create legal personality can be remedied if such an intention can be inferred.

2. Objective Theory

An alternative theory about international legal personality of international organizations goes one step further and suggests that legal personality can be deduced not from the will of the founders, but from the possession of certain attributes by the body itself.[27] This is closer to the manner in which states come into being, with recognition of, say, Kosovo, regarded as being consequent to rather than constitutive of its existence.[28] This makes sense in the context of states coming into being — there is, in fact, a treaty definition of what a state is[29] — but it is less clear when an international organization reaches "organizationhood".[30]

The International Law Commission has not dealt directly with the question of which international organizations enjoy international legal personality; instead its draft articles on the responsibility of international organizations simply assume that international responsibility only applies to organizations "established by a treaty or other instrument governed by international law and possessing its own international legal personality".[31] Similarly, the Vienna Convention on the Law of Treaties Between States and International Organizations or Between International Organizations notes in the preamble "that international organizations possess the capacity to conclude treaties, which is necessary for the exercise of their functions and the fulfilment of their purposes".[32] Both reproduce the essentially circular logic from the *Reparations* case: personality can be deduced from the powers given to an international organization, with the extent of certain powers being deduced in turn from the fact of personality.

A final consideration in this abstract consideration of international legal personality is that it is not plenary — in other words, even if international legal personality is found to exist, that does not conclude the inquiry of what powers such an entity may in fact exercise. In the *Reparations* case, the ICJ noted that:

> the Court has come to the conclusion that the Organization is an international person. That is not the same thing as saying that it is a State, which it certainly is not, or that its legal personality and rights and duties are the same as those of a State. Still less is it the same thing as saying that it is "a super-State", whatever that expression may mean.... Whereas a State possesses the totality of international rights and duties recognized by international law, the rights and duties of an entity such as the Organization must depend upon its purposes and functions as specified or implied in its constituent documents and developed in practice.[33]

ASEAN's Personality

In the case of ASEAN, the reasoning from the *Reparations* case is easily extended to ASEAN with respect to the members themselves: ASEAN enjoys such legal personality as those members have endowed it.[34] But the question of whether states and other actors outside ASEAN must recognize it depends on the application of a more objective set of standards. Though there is no consensus in the literature and little authority from courts (primarily focused on the status of the EU and the OSCE),[35] Ian Brownlie has developed a three-part test summarizing the majority views on international legal personality. To enjoy personality, he argues, an organization must possess the following three attributes:

1. A permanent association of states, with lawful objects, equipped with organs;
2. A distinction, in terms or legal powers and purposes, between the organization and its member states;
3. The existence of legal powers exercisable on the international plane and not solely within the national systems of one or more states.[36]

Applying Brownlie's test, does ASEAN have personality?

1. Permanent Association

The first leg is easily satisfied: even before adopting the Charter, ASEAN was certainly a permanent association of states, with lawful objects, equipped with at least rudimentary organs from the outset, growing into a secretariat over time.[37]

2. Distinction between Organization and Members

Is there, secondly, a distinction, in terms or legal powers and purposes, between the organization and its member states? Traditionally within ASEAN, the answer would have been "no". ASEAN's foundational document, the Bangkok Declaration, essentially stated some shared goals and announced an annual meeting of foreign ministers.[38]

As Tommy Koh and others have argued, the purpose of the Charter is to make ASEAN a more rules-based organization: "The 'ASEAN Way' of relying on networking, consultation, mutual accommodation and consensus will not be done away with. It will be supplemented by a new culture of adherence to rules."[39] This point was emphasized also in the Report of the Eminent Persons Group, which explicitly linked rule-adherence to legal personality.[40] Whether the ASEAN Way, epitomized by *musjawarah* [consultation] and *mufukat* [consensus],[41] is compatible with a rules-based organization will be a key challenge to the organization in years to come.[42] In specific areas, however, there has already been some movement.

In the economic sphere, for example, one might argue that ASEAN has a competence distinct from its members. The Framework Agreement for Enhancing ASEAN Economic Cooperation, for example, has provided the basis for agreements on trade liberalization, industrial cooperation, and foreign direct investment.[43] The possibility of majority voting was considered in the 1996 Protocol on Dispute Settlement Mechanism for ASEAN economic agreements.[44] This was never implemented, but was superseded in 2004 by another protocol that went further in providing for a "negative consensus" model under which the Senior Economic Officials Meeting (SEOM) would have to decide by consensus *not* to set up a panel, adopt a panel report, adopt an appeal report, or authorize retaliation.[45]

A second area in which there have been interesting developments is on nuclear weapons. This is marginal to the day-to-day operations of ASEAN, but the adoption of the Southeast Asia Nuclear-Weapon-Free Zone Treaty in 1995 was unusual for two reasons.[46] This is the treaty that established SEANWFZ (pronounced "*see-yan-fez*"[47] or "*shaun-fizz*"[48]). First, the treaty required only seven ratifications from the ten states parties to enter into force.[49] The treaty would not bind states who had not ratified, but this led to the Philippines sitting in on SEANWFZ meetings as an observer from 1997 until it became a party in June 2001.[50] Secondly, the commission that was established by the treaty provided for decisions to be made by two-thirds majority in cases where consensus could not be reached.[51] The provision has never been implemented and it is unlikely that any matter will be put to a vote.

Other agreements, such as the ASEAN Agreement on Transboundary Haze Pollution, have repeated the limited ratification requirement (in that case lowering it to six),[52] but majority voting in other areas was rejected in the discussions on the ASEAN Charter. Insofar as ASEAN continues to rely on consensus, where every member effectively has a veto, it begs the question of whether the collectivity genuinely has a separate personality from its members. Outside these two areas of economic cooperation and nuclear weapons, there has been little indication of a willingness to grant any form of independence to the organization *qua* organization, with active resistance to such a development in the area of human rights.

3. Powers

Thirdly, does ASEAN possess legal powers exercisable on the international plane and not solely within the national systems of one or more of its states? ASEAN was finally granted observer status at the UN in December 2006,[53] though it was beaten to this milestone by the Asian-African Legal Consultative Organization in 1980,[54] the Asian Development Bank in 2002,[55] and the Shanghai Cooperation Organization and the South Asian Association for Regional Cooperation in 2004.[56]

This means little. A more important test is whether the organization can create and accept legal obligations. The clearest example would be if the organization can enter into treaties in its own right.

The 1979 Agreement Between the Government of Indonesia and ASEAN Relating to the Privileges and Immunities of the ASEAN Secretariat was signed by the Secretary-General of ASEAN, but related only to its status within Indonesia.[57] When outside Indonesia,

ASEAN officials travel as nationals of their respective member states.[58] ASEAN has signed various Memoranda of Understanding (MOUs) such as the 2000 MOU with Australia on Haze,[59] a 2002 MOU with China on Agricultural Cooperation,[60] and a 2003 MOU with China on Information Communications Technology,[61] but on matters regarded as important or that bind the member states, the various members have signed and ratified in their individual capacities.[62]

This appears likely to continue under the Charter. Though the Eminent Persons Group recommended that the Secretary-General be "delegated the authority to sign non-sensitive agreements on behalf of ASEAN Member States",[63] the Charter as adopted merely provides that "ASEAN may conclude agreements with countries" and other entities, with the procedures for concluding such agreements to be prescribed by the ASEAN Coordinating Council in consultation with the Community Councils.[64]

So what does this mean in terms of ASEAN's international legal personality? The first thing to note is that personality at the international level is not so much a status as a capacity. It matters less what you claim than what you do. And, importantly, at the international level there are degrees of legal personality. The UN Charter does not assert personality, but there is no doubt today that the organization possesses it. The ASEAN Charter asserts personality, but ASEAN would appear to have a very limited form of international legal personality already. From the watered-down provisions of the Charter, it is not clear that its ratification will radically alter that analysis of substance as opposed to form.

This was evident in the media release that accompanied the signing of the Charter. Noting that the Charter conferred on ASEAN international legal personality distinct from the member states, the release went on to note that, "Details of what ASEAN can or cannot do with its legal personality will be discussed and stated in a supplementary protocol after the signing of the Charter."[65] Those details will answer the question of whether ASEAN exists in a meaningful sense as an international legal person. By all indications, we will be waiting some time.

DOES ASEAN MATTER?

The question of international legal personality is, in many ways, a theoretical one. As indicated, the contours of that personality remain to be defined. An important factor will be the political environment within which ASEAN operates — in the sense of the willingness of members to cede powers to the centre, and of non-members to deal with that centre. What, then, is the practical significance of ASEAN?

Is ASEAN More than the Sum of Its Parts? Or Less?

Is ASEAN more than the sum of its parts? When ASEAN was created, the answer would probably have been no. The Bangkok Declaration merely laid the basis for a regular meeting with a skeletal institutional structure. Whether it has grown beyond that depends on whom one is asking, with a fairly clear distinction between the views of ASEAN's members and aspiring members, and those with whom it has external dealings.

1. Among ASEAN Members

For its members and those who wish to join it, the significance of ASEAN has changed over time. First, ASEAN has seen the gradual emergence of an identity, justified in large part as a means of linking economies but incidentally establishing regular lines of communication for political, economic and socio-cultural relations. Secondly, its embryonic institutions have grown into more regular contacts and a framework for more formal discussion of multilateral issues.

The Charter formalizes both these trends, more clearly articulating a shared vision for the region and strengthening some of the institutions. On the "vision", it outlines broad if vague support

for peace, stability, justice, democracy, and prosperity, with far
more concrete purposes articulated in the economic sphere:

> To create a single market and production base which is stable,
> prosperous, highly competitive and economically integrated with
> effective facilitation for trade and investment in which there is
> free flow of goods, services and investment; facilitated movement
> of business persons, professionals, talents and labour; and freer
> flow of capital.[66]

On institutions, the Charter makes the ASEAN Summit bi-annual
rather than annual, establishes the meeting of foreign ministers as
a Coordinating Council, provides single chairs for high-level ASEAN
bodies, calls for the appointment of permanent representatives,
and creates three "community councils" in the areas of political and
security, economic, and socio-cultural affairs — as well as an
undefined "human rights body".[67]

At the same time, however, the Charter reaffirms consultation
and consensus as a "basic principle".[68] Where consensus cannot
be achieved, the ASEAN Summit may decide on how a specific
decision can be made.[69] If there is a serious breach of the Charter
or non-compliance, the matter will be referred to the ASEAN
Summit for decision.[70]

It remains unclear how much significance the Charter will have
on what ASEAN does and how, but three points are worth
highlighting as possible drivers of real change. The first is the
opening up of a possible two-track (or perhaps multi-track) "ASEAN
Minus X" formula for economic cooperation.[71] This could strengthen
ASEAN by allowing deeper ties between some members, or it
could destroy ASEAN by fragmentation.

The second is that ASEAN's Chairman and Secretary-General
can be requested to provide good offices, conciliation or mediation
in a dispute.[72] A useful comparison may be made with the Secretary-
General of the UN. Initially conceived as more "secretary" than
"general", the position is described in the UN Charter as the

organization's "chief administrative officer". This has grown over time as various incumbents have expanded the role to become a major diplomatic and political actor in its own right.[73]

The third is the discussion about a human rights body. Though it is unlikely that anything comparable to the European Court of Human Rights is likely to be established, the discussion itself has been interesting. As Singapore's Foreign Minister George Yeo observed, there has been disagreement among the members on what form the human rights entity should take, driven in part by fears that Western countries and non-governmental organizations (NGOs) will use it to interfere in domestic politics. The end result of having a "body" was an attempt to placate such concerns, though he gently suggested that though such a body may end up lacking teeth, it "will at least have a tongue and a tongue will have its uses".[74] With the formalization of the position of Secretary-General and the appointment of Surin Pitsuwan, it is possible that a strong Secretary-General could assume responsibility for that tongue.

2. ASEAN's External Relations

So within ASEAN there is some reason for cautious optimism. Outside ASEAN, however, there is an argument that the body is in fact less than the sum of its parts. Tommy Koh has cited two recent examples of policy-makers in Washington and Brussels not appearing to take ASEAN particularly seriously:

> At the Williamsburg Conference, held in Mongolia in June 2007, I was distressed to hear a senior US official say: "the ASEAN way is no way." At the ASEAN-US Symposium, held in October 2007 in Singapore, I was astonished to hear another senior U.S. official say that he had personally advised Secretary Rice, not once but twice, not to attend the annual ASEAN Regional Forum (ARF). I suspect the same attitude prevails in Brussels. This could explain why ministerial meetings between ASEAN and the EU are often attended by full ministers on the ASEAN side, but not on the EU side.[75]

To many outside observers ASEAN as an international organization is useful if it binds together the ten members and promotes peace and development, but unless and until it offers something more, then liaising directly with ASEAN does not reduce the need for bilateral diplomacy with the various states. All it does is to add another layer of diplomacy. This is not helped by debacles such as the aborted briefing by UN special envoy Ibrahim Gambari on Myanmar at the ASEAN Summit in 2007.[76]

There are some exceptions to the general rule that ASEAN is not a good interlocutor with external actors, though this tends to be through separate institutions: such as the way in which ASEAN+3 has come to be used as a forum to discuss financial coordination and territorial disputes in the South China Sea, or that the ARF is now used as an informal platform for security dialogue between twenty-three states.[77]

So in essence, the answer to the question of whether ASEAN matters is probably "yes" to the ten member states, but to everyone else, the honest answer would be "not much".

To What Should We Compare ASEAN?

Underlying all of this is the question of what ASEAN is meant to be. In particular, is it fair or accurate or helpful to compare it to the UN or the EU? Is that the right test? One might argue, for example, that traditional conceptions of legal personality depend on a notion of sovereignty that is not shared in Asia (or at least Southeast Asia). Instead "non-legalized" informal institutions are the hallmark of this region, though they can also be seen as exemplars of the new phenomenon of trans-governmental networks that play an increasingly important role in global governance decisions.[78]

Even so, there are still useful comparisons to be drawn. But the UN and the EU are the wrong ones. Closer might be the origins of the OAS, or perhaps even more aptly, the Conference on Security and Cooperation in Europe (CSCE), which laid the foundations for today's OSCE. ASEAN may well be best understood as a kind of standing diplomatic conference, which is currently talking about becoming something more. Indeed, there is something of an irony that just as ASEAN may become Asia's first truly "legalized" international organization, the CSCE was originally decried as a deplorable departure from legalization with its unenforceable human rights provisions.[79] Despite the scorn of Western international relations scholars, however, dissidents were later able to co-opt the language of such documents to call for union rights in Poland, *glasnost* in Russia, and, after 1989, multi-party elections.[80] These weak norms provided a language for the articulation of rights that later transformed societies. It would be overly optimistic to suggest that the ASEAN Charter will have comparable effects, but changing even the language of international affairs in Southeast Asia is a significant advance on the "Asian values" debates of the 1990s.

Theory also has useful contributions to make, provided we think broadly rather than narrowly. In particular, it may be helpful to understand "institution" not in the narrow sense of legal personality, but in the larger sense of that word used by international relations scholars, denoting "persistent and connected sets of rules (formal or informal) that prescribe behavioural roles, constrain activity, and shape expectations".[81] In that larger sense ASEAN would certainly appear to be an "institution". ASEAN's achievements are not that it is the foundation of an Asian Union to rival the EU, but more modestly that it fosters peace, encourages development, and promotes human rights in a part of the world that needs all three of these things.[82]

CONCLUSION

In Molière's *Le Bourgeois gentilhomme*, M. Jourdain is a foolish member of the middle-class who aspires to join the aristocracy. He orders splendid new clothes and aspires, unsuccessfully, to learning the gentlemanly arts of fencing, dancing, music, and philosophy.

His philosophy lesson degenerates into a basic lesson on language and rhetoric in which he seeks to learn prose and is startled to discover that he has been speaking it all his life.[83]

To return to the question with which this chapter opened, and with the assistance of another French author, we might then conclude that ASEAN has always existed and that its problem is not legal personality but a shared vision of the purpose of that existence, of its place in the world. The Charter process, as important as it was, merely deferred most of these questions.

Notes

This chapter also appears in the *Singapore Yearbook of International Law* (2008). The author thanks Robert C. Beckman, Koh Kheng-Lian, Lim Chin Leng, Victor Ramraj, and an anonymous reviewer for their comments on an earlier draft and to Ana Christina Flores for invaluable research assistance on this project. He may be contacted at chesterman@nyu.edu.

 1. Jean Baudrillard, *The Gulf War Never Happened* (Oxford: Polity Press, 1995).
 2. Association of Southeast Asian Nations, *The ASEAN Declaration*, Indonesia, Malaysia, Philippines, Singapore and Thailand, Bangkok, 8 August 1967, available at <http://www.aseansec.org/1212.htm> [*Bangkok Declaration*].
 3. Teresa Whitfield, *Friends Indeed? The United Nations, Groups of Friends, and the Resolution of Conflict* (Washington, D.C.: United States Institute of Peace Press, 2007).
 4. *Charter of the United Nations*, 26 June 1945, 892 UNTS 993 (entered into force 24 October 1945), especially Chapter VII.
 5. Rodolfo Severino, "Asia Policy Lecture: What ASEAN Is and What It Stands For", The Research Institute for Asia and the Pacific, University of Sydney, Australia, 22 October 1998, available at <http://www.aseansec.org/3399.htm>.
 6. Rodolfo Severino, "Introduction", in *Framing the ASEAN Charter: An ISEAS Perspective*, edited by Rodolfo Severino (Singapore: Institute of Southeast Asian Studies, 2005), p. 3 at 6. In the same volume, Locknie Hsu adopted a more nuanced position that ASEAN's legal personality needed "clarification". Locknie Hsu, "Towards an ASEAN Charter: Some Thoughts from the Legal Perspective", p. 45. *Cf.* Seiji Naya, et al., *ASEAN Economic Cooperation for the 1990s: A Report Prepared for the ASEAN Standing Committee* (Manila: Philippine Institute for Development Studies, 1992), p. 112 (concluding that ASEAN has a "nascent international legal personality"); JiangYu Wang, "International Legal Personality of ASEAN and the Legal Nature of the China-ASEAN Free Trade Agreement", in *China-ASEAN Relations: Economic and Legal Dimensions*, edited by John Wong, Zou Keyuan, and Zeng Huaqun (Singapore: World Scientific, 2006), p. 111 at 126 (ASEAN has "selective personality").
 7. Paul Davidson, *ASEAN: The Evolving Legal Framework for Economic Cooperation* (Singapore: Times Academic Press, 2002), p. 29.

8. *Charter of the Association of Southeast Asian Nations,* 20 November 2007 (entered into force 15 December 2008), Article 3, available at <http://www.aseansec.org/AC.htm> [*ASEAN Charter*].

9. Ibid., Article 47(4).

10. Ian Brownlie, *Principles of Public International Law,* 5th ed. (Oxford: Clarendon Press, 1998), p. 57. See generally Janne Elisabeth Nijman, *The Concept of International Legal Personality: An Inquiry into the History and Theory of International Law* (The Hague: TMC Asser Press, 2004).

11. See, for example, *Charter of the United Nations,* Article 2, paras. 4 and 7.

12. Statute of the International Court of Justice, 26 June 1945, UNTS 993 (entered into force 24 October 1945), Article 34(1). *Cf. Mavrommatis Palestine Concessions (Greece v. United Kingdom)* (1924) PCIJ (Ser. A) No. 2, pp. 10, 12 (Aug. 30) (allowing the Greek government to sue on behalf of a Greek national).

13. Thus the *Charter of the United Nations,* Article 104 provides that "The Organization shall enjoy in the territory of each of its Members such legal capacity as may be necessary for the exercise of its functions and the fulfilment of its purposes." This does not answer the question of the international legal personality of the United Nations.

14. See, for example, Konstantinos D. Magliverasa and Gino J. Naldia, "The African Union — A New Dawn for Africa?" *Int'l & Comp LQ* 51 (2002): 415 (suggesting that the OAU's international legal personality could be inferred from a provision comparable to UN Charter, Article 104).

15. See, for example, International Agreement on Olive Oil and Table Olives, 29 April 2005, TD.OLIVE OIL.10/6 (entered into force 25 May 2007), Article 5(1), available at <http://www.internationaloliveoil.org/downloads/Convenio03eng.pdf>. ("The International Olive Council shall have international legal personality. It shall, in particular, have the capacity to contract, to acquire and dispose of moveable and immoveable property and to institute legal proceedings. It shall not have the power to borrow money.")

16. Reparation for Injuries Suffered in the Service of the United Nations, Advisory Opinion, (1949) ICJ Rep. 174 [*Reparations* case], p. 179.

17. Israel joined the United Nations in May 1949, a month after the Court issued its advisory opinion.

18. *Reparations* case, supra note 16 at 185 [emphasis added].

19. United Nations Convention on the Law of the Sea, 10 December 1982, 1833 UNTS 3 (entered into force 16 November 1994), Article 176, available at <http://www.un.org/Depts/los> [UNCLOS]. ("The Authority shall have international legal personality and such legal capacity as may be necessary for the exercise of its functions and the fulfilment of its purposes.")

20. Rome Statute of the International Criminal Court, 17 July 1998, 2187 UNTS 90, UN Doc A/Conf.183/9 (entered into force 1 July 2002), Article 4, available at <http://www.icc-cpi.int/library/about/officialjournal/Rome_Statute_120704-EN.pdf> [*Rome Statute*]. ("The Court shall have international legal personality.")

21. International Agreement on Olive Oil and Table Olives, supra note 15, Article 5(1) ("The International Olive Council shall have international legal personality. It shall, in particular, have the capacity to contract, to acquire and dispose of moveable and immoveable

property and to institute legal proceedings. It shall not have the power to borrow money."). Other examples include:

— the Western Indian Ocean Tuna Organisation: *Convention on the Western Indian Ocean Tuna Organisation*, 19 June 1991, Article 8(1), available at <http://www.fao.org/fi/body/rfb/WIOTO/wioto_convention_text.doc>. ("The Organisation shall have international legal personality and such legal capacity as may be necessary for the exercise of its functions and the fulfilment of its purposes, in particular the capacity to conclude agreements at the international level to contract, to acquire and dispose of moveable and immoveable property and to sue and to be sued in accordance with its legal and diplomatic status.");

— the Caribbean Disaster Emergency Response Agency: *Agreement Establishing the Caribbean Disaster Emergency Response Agency*, September 1991, Article 26(1), available at <http://www.cdera.org/about_cdera_agreement.php>. ("The Agency shall have international legal personality and such legal capacity as may be necessary for the exercise of its functions and the fulfilment of its objectives.");

— the International Sugar Organization: *International Sugar Agreement*, 20 March 1992, [1992] O.J. L379/16, Article 6(1), available at <http://www.isosugar.org/home/agreements/agreementenglish.htm>. ("The Organization shall have international legal personality.");

— the Commission for the Conservation and Management of Highly Migratory Fish Stocks in the Western and Central Pacific Ocean: *Convention on the Conservation and Management of Highly Migratory Fish Stocks in the Western and Central Pacific Ocean*, 5 September 2000, [2005] OJ L32/3 (entered into force 19 June 2004), Article 9(6), available at <http://www.wcpfc.int>. ("The Commission shall have international legal personality and such legal capacity as may be necessary to perform its functions and achieve its objectives.")

22. *Charter of Shanghai Cooperation Organisation*, China, Kazakhstan, Kyrgyzstan, Russian Federation, Tajikistan and Uzbekistan, 7 June 2002, Article 15, available at <http://www.sectsco.org/news_detail.asp?id=96&LanguageID=2>.

23. Philippe Gautier, "The Reparation for Injuries Case Revisited: The Personality of the European Union", *Max Planck Y.B. United Nations L.* (2000): 331; Rafael Leal-Arcas, "EU Legal Personality in Foreign Policy?" *BU Int'l LJ* 24 (2006): 165.

24. Treaty of Lisbon Amending the Treaty on European Union and the Treaty Establishing the European Community, 13 December 2007, (not yet in force), Article 1(55), available at <http://europa.eu/lisbon_treaty> (inserting new Article 46A into the Treaty on European Union).

25. Magliverasa and Naldia, supra note 14.

26. Charter of the Organization of American States, 30 April 1948, 119 UNTS 3 (entered into force 13 December 1951), available at <http://www.oas.org/juridico/english/charter.html>.

27. See, for example, Rosalyn Higgins, *Problems and Process: International Law and How We Use It* (Oxford: Clarendon Press, 1994), p. 48.

28. Christopher J. Borgen, "Kosovo's Declaration of Independence: Self-Determination, Secession and Recognition", ASIL Insights 12, Issue 2 (2008), available at <http://www.asil.org/insights080229.cfm>.

29. Montevideo Convention on the Rights and Duties of States, 26 December 1933, OASTS 37 (entered into force 26 December 1934), available at <http://en.wikisource.org/wiki/Montevideo_Convention>.

30. See generally Jan Klabbers, *An Introduction to International Institutional Law* (Cambridge: Cambridge University Press, 2002), pp. 42–59; Philippe Sands and Pierre Klein, *Bowett's Law of International Institutions*, 5th ed. (London: Sweet & Maxwell, 2001), pp. 469–531; José Alvarez, *International Organizations as Law-makers* (Oxford: Oxford University Press, 2005), pp. 129–39. *Cf.* Giorgio Gaja, *First Report on Responsibility of International Organizations*, UN Doc A/CN.4/532 (2003), available at <http://www.un.org/law/ilc>, para. 19: "Even if a treaty provision were intended to confer international personality on a particular organization, the acquisition of legal personality would depend on the actual establishment of the organization. It is clear that an organization merely existing on paper cannot be considered a subject of international law. The entity further needs to have acquired a sufficient independence from its members so that it cannot be regarded as acting as an organ common to the members. When such an independent entity comes into being, one could speak of an "objective international personality", as the court did in its advisory opinion on Reparation for injuries suffered in the service of the United Nations. The characterization of an organization as a subject of international law thus appears as a question of fact. Although the view has been expressed that an organization's personality exists with regard to non-member states only if they have recognized it, this assumption cannot be regarded as a logical necessity" [footnotes omitted].

31. International Law Commission, *Draft Articles on Responsibility of International Organizations provisionally adopted by the International Law Commission at its fifty-eighth session*, UN Doc A/58/10 (2003), pp. 38–45, available at <http://www.un.org/law/ilc>. International organizations, as understood by the ILC, "may include as members, in addition to States, other entities". As to the theoretical foundation of such organizations international legal personality, the ILC has observed that the ICJ "appeared to favour the view that when legal personality of an organization exists, it is an 'objective' personality. Thus, it would not be necessary to enquire whether the legal personality of an organization has been recognized by an injured state before considering whether the organization may be held internationally responsible according to the present draft articles. On the other hand, an organization merely existing on paper could not be considered as having an 'objective' legal personality under international law." Ibid., p. 42.

32. Vienna Convention on the Law of Treaties Between States and International Organizations or Between International Organizations, 21 March 1986, (not yet in force), preamble, available at <http://untreaty.un.org/ilc/texts/instruments/english/conventions/1_2_1986.pdf> [VCLTIO]. *Cf.* Article 6: "The capacity of an international organization to conclude treaties is governed by the rules of that organization."

33. *Reparations* case, supra note 16.

34. See Henry G. Schermers and Niels M. Blokker, *International Institutional Law: Unity Within Diversity*, 4th ed. (Leiden: Martinus Nijhoff, 2003), pp. 989–93.

35. Ibid., pp. 991–93.

36. Brownlie, supra note 10, pp. 679–80. Other tests are, of course, possible.

37. ASEAN has developed an extensive network of national actors, but the reference here is to the limited independent organs that exist. It is indicative that ASEAN officials travel on their own national passports.

38. Bangkok Declaration, supra note 2.

39. Tommy Koh, Walter Woon, and Chan Sze-Wei, "Charter Makes ASEAN Stronger, More United and Effective", *Straits Times* [of Singapore], 8 August 2007.

40. The Eminent Persons Group on the ASEAN Charter, *Report of the Eminent Persons Group on the ASEAN Charter* (Jakarta, December 2006), para. 43: "By embarking on building the ASEAN Community, ASEAN has clearly signalled its commitment to move from an Association towards a more structured Intergovernmental Organisation, in the context of legally binding rules and agreements. In this regard, ASEAN should have legal personality." Available at <http://www.aseansec.org/19247.pdf> [Eminent Persons Group, *Report*].

41. See Zakirul Hafez, *The Dimensions of Regional Trade Integration in Southeast Asia* (Ardsley, NY: Transnational Publishers, 2004), pp. 119–23.

42. *Cf.* Koh Kheng-Lian and Nicholas Robinson, "Strengthening Sustainable Development in Regional Inter-Governmental Governance: Lessons from the ASEAN Way", *Singapore J Int'l Comp L* 6 (2002): 640; Koh Kheng-Lian, "ASEAN Environmental Protection in Natural Resources and Sustainable Development: Convergence Versus Divergence?" *Macquarie J Int'l Comp Envt'l L* 4 (2007): 43 at 45.

43. See Paul Davidson, "The ASEAN Way and Role of Law in ASEAN Economic Cooperation", *Singapore YB Int'l L* 8 (2004): 165 at 158–61.

44. ASEAN Protocol on Dispute Settlement Mechanism, 20 November 1996 (entered into force 26 May 1998), available at <http://www.aseansec.org/16654.htm>.

45. ASEAN Protocol on Enhanced Dispute Settlement Mechanism, 29 November 2004 (entered into force 29 November 2004), Articles 5(1), 9(1), 12(13), 16(6), 16(8), available at <http://www.aseansec.org/16754.htm>; Rodolfo Severino, *Southeast Asia in Search of an ASEAN Community: Insights from the Former ASEAN Secretary-General* (Singapore: Institute of Southeast Asian Studies, 2006), p. 35 [Severino, *Southeast Asia*]; Joel Vander Kooi, "The ASEAN Enhanced Dispute Settlement Mechanism", *N Int'l L Rev* 20 (2007): 1. I am grateful to Lim Chin Leng for his thoughtful comments on this aspect of ASEAN's legal personality.

46. Southeast Asia Nuclear Weapon-Free Zone Treaty, 15 December 1995 (entered into force 28 March 1997), available at <http://www.aseansec.org/2082.htm> [*Bangkok Treaty*].

47. Johnna Villaviray-Giolagon, "SEANWFZ", *Manila Times*, 28 February 2007.

48. Severino, *Southeast Asia*, supra note 45 at 16.

49. Bangkok Treaty, supra note 46, Article 16(1). At the time of signing, Myanmar, Laos, and Cambodia had not yet joined ASEAN.

50. Severino, *Southeast Asia*, supra note 45, p. 17.
51. Bangkok Treaty, supra note 46, Article 8(8).
52. ASEAN Agreement on Transboundary Haze Pollution, 10 June 2002 (entered into force 11 November 2003), Article 29(1), available at <http://www.aseansec.org/6086.htm>. (Indonesia has yet to ratify the agreement.) See also Agreement on the Establishment of the ASEAN Centre for Biodiversity, 12 September 2005, available at <http://www.aseansec.org/acb_copy.pdf> (six ratifications required); Protocol 1 — Designation of Transit Transport Routes and Facilities and its Annex of List of Transit Transport Routes, 8 February 2007, available at <http://www.aseansec.org/19734.htm> (six ratifications required).
53. GA Res 61/44 (2006).
54. GA Res 35/2 (1980).
55. GA Res 57/30 (2002).
56. GA Res 59/48 (2004); GA Res 59/53 (2004).
57. Agreement Between the Government of Indonesia and ASEAN Relating to the Privileges and Immunities of the ASEAN Secretariat, 20 January 1979 (entered into force 22 March 1979), available at <http://www.aseansec.org/1268.htm>.
58. Naya, supra note 6, p. 112.
59. Memorandum of Understanding (MOU) between the Association of South East Asian Nations (ASEAN) and the Commonwealth of Australia (on Haze), 28 January 2000, available at <http://www.aseansec.org/670.htm>.
60. Memorandum of Understanding Between the Association of Southeast Asian Nations (ASEAN) Secretariat and the Ministry of Agriculture of the People's Republic of China on Agricultural Cooperation, 2 November 2002, available at <http://www.aseansec.org/13214.htm>.
61. Memorandum of Understanding Between the Association of Southeast Asian Nations and the People's Republic of China on Cooperation in Information and Communications Technology, 8 October 2003, available at <http://www.aseansec.org/15147.htm>.
62. See, for example, Framework Agreement on Comprehensive Economic Co-Operation Between ASEAN and the People's Republic of China, 5 November 2002, available at <http://www.aseansec.org/13196.htm>, referring to "the Heads of Government/State of Brunei Darussalam, the Kingdom of Cambodia, the Republic of Indonesia, [etc] ..., Member States of the Association of South East Asian Nations (collectively, 'ASEAN' or 'ASEAN Member States', or individually, 'ASEAN Member State') ...".
63. Eminent Persons Group, *Report*, supra note 40, para. 37.
64. ASEAN Charter, supra note 8, Article 41(7).
65. ASEAN Secretariat, Media Release, "ASEAN Leaders Sign ASEAN Charter", 20 November 2007, available at <http://www.aseansec.org/21085.htm>.
66. ASEAN Charter, supra note 8, Article 1(5).
67. Ibid.
68. Ibid., Article 20(1).
69. Ibid., Article 20(2).

70. Ibid., Article 20(4).

71. Ibid., Article 21(2). The "X" denotes the possibility that one or more members might not opt in to a specific area of economic cooperation.

72. Ibid., Article 23(2).

73. See generally Simon Chesterman, ed., *Secretary or General? The UN Secretary-General in World Politics* (Cambridge: Cambridge University Press, 2007).

74. George Yeo, "Remarks by Minister for Foreign Affairs George Yeo and his reply to supplementary questions in Parliament during CoS debate (MFA)", Ministry of Foreign Affairs, Singapore, 28 February 2008, para. 11, available at <http://app.mfa.gov.sg/2006/press/view_press.asp?post_id=3768>.

75. Tommy Koh, "ASEAN at 40: Perception and Reality", *Pacific Forum CSIS*, 27 November 2007, available at <http://www.csis.org/media/csis/pubs/pac0748a.pdf> [Koh, "ASEAN at 40"]. *Cf.* Catharin E. Dalpino, *New Power Dynamics in Southeast Asia* (Muscatine, IA: The Stanley Foundation, September 2008), available at <http://www.stanley foundation.org/resources.cfm?id=347>.

76. "UN Envoy Won't Address ASEAN Summit After Myanmar Objects", *International Herald Tribune*, 19 November 2007.

77. Mark Beeson, "Multilateralism, American Power and East Asian Regionalism", Southeast Asia Research Centre Working Papers Series no. 64 (2004), available at <http://www.cityu.edu.hk/searc/WP64_04_Beeson.pdf>.

78. Miles Kahler, "Legalization as Strategy: The Asia-Pacific Case", *Int'l Org* 54, Issue 3 (2000): 549; Anne-Marie Slaughter, *A New World Order* (Princeton: Princeton University Press, 2004).

79. Daniel C. Thomas, *The Helsinki Effect: International Norms, Human Rights, and the Demise of Communism* (Princeton, NJ: Princeton University Press, 2001), pp. 244–55.

80. Michael Ignatieff, "Human Rights, Power, and the State", in *Making States Work: State Failure and the Crisis of Governance*, edited by Simon Chesterman, Michael Ignatieff and Ramesh Thakur (Tokyo: United Nations University Press, 2005), p. 59 at 62.

81. Robert O. Keohane, "International Institutions: Two Approaches", *Int'l Stud Q* 32 (1988): 379 at 383.

82. *Cf.* Tommy Koh's list of ASEAN achievements: keeping the region peaceful, maintaining strategic sea lanes, laying the foundations of a single market, promoting multiculturalism, and providing a basic architecture for multilateralism: Koh, "ASEAN at 40", supra note 75 at 40.

83. I am grateful to Anne-Marie Slaughter for first noting the similarity between Molière and Asian approaches to trans-governmental networks.

SUMMARY OF KEY POINTS

S. Tiwari

Article 3 of the ASEAN Charter provides that "ASEAN as an inter-governmental organisation, is hereby conferred legal personality." This chapter examined the legal status of ASEAN and the political question of whether the whole was greater or less than the sum of its parts.

(a) International Legal Personality: An Issue of Status or Capacity?

In examining the legal status and the political question, it was argued that legal personality at the international level was less a status than a capacity. Further, the fact that ASEAN now claimed international legal personality in the Charter did not necessarily mean that it lacked it previously, nor that it now possessed it in any meaningful way. Rather, the key question, in the author's view, was what specific powers had been granted to ASEAN and how those powers are used.

(b) ASEAN in Legal Terms: The Contours Continue to be Refined

The writer next dealt with the question: what is ASEAN in international legal terms? It is clear that it is more than just a group of friends, ten states that share a set of interests and goals. At the same time it cannot compare itself to the United Nations (UN), an international organization that asserts the power to impose binding obligations on all states. It is more than an annual meeting of foreign ministers hoping to promote economic growth, but less than the World Trade Organization (WTO). Of the world's significant regional organizations, the powers ceded by members to the centre are less than within the European Union (EU), the African Union (AU), or the Organization of American States (OAS). Yet within Asia, it is perhaps the most important regional organization, with a wider mandate than the Asia-Pacific Economic Cooperation forum (APEC) and deeper commitments than the Shanghai Cooperation Organization (SCO).

He explained that in considering the issue of ASEAN in international legal terms, it is instructive to consider whether there will now be a distinction — in terms of legal powers and purposes — between the organization and its member states.The Charter is intended to make ASEAN a more rules-based organization, though the "ASEAN Way" of relying on networking, consultation, mutual accommodation and consensus will continue. Whether the "ASEAN Way" is compatible with a rules-based organization will be an important challenge for ASEAN in the years to come. A point to note in this connection, however, is that there have been steps to get around the consensus rule in certain areas.

(c) Does ASEAN Exist: The Charter's Intriguing Article 41(7)

The Charter has an intriguing provision in Article 41(7). It reads:

> ASEAN may conclude agreements with countries or sub-regional, regional and international organisations and institutions. The procedures for concluding such agreements shall be prescribed by the ASEAN Coordinating Council in consultation with the ASEAN Community Councils.

The chapter raised the question whether Article 41(7) will give rise to an ASEAN entity able to act independently of its members. The work to operationalize Article 41(7) has still not been done. Thus one has to wait to see how the provision will be implemented.

LEGAL PERSONALITY AND RELATED MATTERS EXPLAINED

S. Tiwari

This section covers issues which surfaced in the discussion following the presentations on legal personality.

Legality of Contracts Entered into in Indonesia by the Secretary-General of ASEAN

It was clarified that such contracts were valid, as the ASEAN Secretariat had the capacity, *inter alia*, to conclude contracts under the agreement between Indonesia and ASEAN governments relating to privileges and immunities of the ASEAN Secretariat.

Drafting was Technical and Implementation was Political

In the context of a discussion that ASEAN countries tended to delay ratification and implementation of agreements, a view was expressed that this was because in ASEAN drafting a treaty was taken to be a technical exercise for the officials. However, it was up to the governments of the countries to decide when they would ratify and whether they would implement the agreements, implementation being political in nature. It was pointed out that drafting was political too as what went into the treaties was based on the mandate given to the ASEAN officials by each of their governments. The governments should not drag their feet on ratification and implementation after having negotiated a treaty. It was this tendency to delay ratification and implementation that had given ASEAN a bad name.

The European Community Experience

Two interesting points were shared. One, it was pointed out that states followed rules because they wanted to and because it was in their interest to do so, and not because they had to. In the European Union (EU) if a member state did not act in conformity with community law, the EU Commission would lodge a case at the EU Court of Justice. This would always lead the member state to comply or work towards a political negotiation to sort out the matter in issue. Two, it was argued that in vesting a regional entity with powers, the states had not surrendered their sovereignty, as was popularly thought. They could not do that without changing their Constitution. What had occurred was a pooling of sovereignty.

The WTO Mechanism Explained

In dealing with the question whether the WTO was a world policeman for trade and, if so, how it enforced its rules, it was explained that the WTO was not intended to act as a policeman but as a system by which members could negotiate. If a party did not comply with commitments, then a process was in place by which grievances could be addressed. If a party was adjudged to have disregarded the applicable rules but still did not work out a mutually acceptable solution, then there was a way in which another state could retaliate without being in breach of the WTO rules.

3

LIFE IN ASEAN AFTER THE ENTRY INTO FORCE OF THE ASEAN CHARTER
Implications and Follow-ups

Termsak Chalermpalanupap

This chapter explores how the ASEAN Charter has changed or will change ASEAN in four areas: (1) democracy; (2) human rights cooperation; (3) becoming a more rules-based organization; and (4) organizational structure. It will not attempt to examine how the Charter is going to change the member states of ASEAN. That important but highly sensitive question will have to be addressed by each member state concerned.

DEMOCRACY IN ASEAN

As an inter-governmental organization, ASEAN is actually very democratic. Just look at the following evidence: sovereign equality as one of the principles (Article 2, Paragraph 2a of the Charter); every member state is equal in representation and participation in ASEAN; annual rotation of the ASEAN chairmanship; no weighted voting right or veto power; decision-making by consultation and consensus; and equal contribution to the annual operational budget of the ASEAN Secretariat, etc.

Sovereign equality begets non-interference.[1] But non-interference cannot be absolute when a state joins a regional grouping like ASEAN and takes part in its community-building endeavour. Hence the Charter includes two new principles: "shared commitment and collective responsibility in enhancing regional peace, security and prosperity" (Article 2, Paragraph 2b) and "enhanced consultations on matters seriously affecting the common interest of ASEAN" (Article 2, Paragraph 2g). All the principles in Article 2 must be accepted and upheld as a whole set. No member state can pick and choose to highlight some principles and ignore the rest.

Unlike the EU, ASEAN has never prescribed any political criteria of its membership. The Charter's Article 6 on Admission of New Members merely lists the following: (a) geographical location in Southeast Asia; (b) recognition by all ASEAN member states; (c) agreement to be bound and to abide by the Charter; and (d) ability and willingness to carry out the obligations of membership.[2]

Consequently, ASEAN may be the only inter-governmental organization in the world with such amazing political diversity. The wide range of political systems among its member states extends from the far left (Laos and Vietnam are ruled by their respective Communist parties), to the far right (Myanmar still has a military-led government, and Brunei Darussalam is a sovereign sultanate), with different types of parliamentary or republican democracies in between. The only other international body with such political diversity is the UN.

Interestingly, the Charter mentions "democracy" and "democratic values" in three sections:

- In the *Preamble*: "Adhering to the principles of democracy, the rule of law and good governance, respect for and protection of human rights and fundamental freedoms";

- In the *Purposes* (of ASEAN): "7. To strengthen democracy, enhance good governance and the rule of law, and to promote and protect human rights and fundamental freedoms, with due regard to the rights and responsibilities of the Member States of ASEAN"; and
- In the *Principles*: "(h) adherence to the rule of law, good governance, the principles of democracy and constitutional government;

  (i) respect for fundamental freedoms, the promotion and protection of human rights, and the promotion of social justice".

Moreover, the ASEAN Charter includes a provision in Article 14 on the establishment of an ASEAN human rights body as a new organ of ASEAN. This issue will be dealt with in the next segment of this chapter. In addition, the Blueprint for the ASEAN Political-Security Community (APSC)[3] includes the following as one of the characteristics and elements of the APSC:

> "The APSC shall promote political development in adherence to the principles of democracy, the rule of law and good governance, respect for and promotion and protection of human rights and fundamental freedoms as inscribed in the ASEAN Charter. ..."

The APSC Blueprint includes in its cooperation in political development three actions under A.1.8 to promote principles of democracy.[4] They are aimed at creating a rules-based community of shared values and norms.

All of the above begs one tough question: How can ASEAN regional cooperation complement national efforts in political development and democratization?

A far less perilous question to explore here is how ASEAN is trying to democratize itself. The answer can be found in the Charter; for example, in Article 1, Paragraph 13, in which ASEAN professes "to promote a people-oriented ASEAN in which all sectors of society are encouraged to participate in, and benefit from, the process of ASEAN integration and community building". Moreover, the Charter includes in Chapter V a commitment to engage with "entities associated with ASEAN" that support the ASEAN Charter, in particular its purposes and principles. These entities, as listed in Annex 2 of the Charter, include parliamentarians in the ASEAN Inter-Parliamentary Assembly (AIPA); business organizations; think-tanks and academic institutions; accredited civil society organizations; and other stakeholders in ASEAN.

The Committee of Permanent Representatives (CPR) based in Jakarta and the Secretary-General of ASEAN as well as the ASEAN Secretariat will be the key focal points for the engagement with these entities. However, such engagement does not necessarily involve direct participation of these entities in ASEAN's decision-making or policy-setting meetings. By its very nature as an inter-governmental organization, ASEAN's membership is at the national government level; ASEAN decisions are made by government representatives of all its member states; ASEAN mechanisms are accountable to member states.

On the other hand, the ASEAN Community that member states are building is intended for their peoples to benefit from. What is envisaged to take shape in Southeast Asia by the year 2015 is a community of caring and sharing ASEAN peoples — not just a collection of more ASEAN meetings of officials, ministers, or leaders.

In order to achieve a win-win outcome, member states and their officials, ministers, and leaders will have to adjust the way they conduct ASEAN cooperation and create new opportunities for peoples to interact with them and participate in their activities. ASEAN peoples, through the entities that they belong, also need to learn more about ASEAN, appreciate its purposes and accept its principles. Top-down leadership has put in place the Charter and the roadmap for community-building. To be sustainable and meaningful, community-building requires public awareness, public support and engagement. ASEAN Community needs its peoples to move beyond a bureaucratic construct and transform into a real life community of peoples.

HUMAN RIGHTS COOPERATION

A crucial test of ASEAN's democracy is in human rights cooperation. This is one critical area in which the human security and well-being of ASEAN peoples are at stake. Article 14 of the Charter calls for the establishment of an "ASEAN human rights body". But one important caveat appears in Paragraph 1 of Article 14: "In conformity with the purposes and principles of the ASEAN Charter relating to the promotion and protection of human rights and fundamental freedoms ...". The other caveat is in Paragraph 2 of Article 14: "This ASEAN human rights body shall operate in accordance with the terms of reference to be determined by the ASEAN Foreign Ministers Meeting [AMM]."

Established at the 41st AMM in Singapore in July 2008, the High Level Panel (HLP) drafting the terms of reference for the ASEAN human rights body has convened thirteen meetings. The HLP plans to meet in Chiangmai from 10–12 July 2009 to try to wrap up the drafting of the terms of reference and to prepare its report to the 42nd AMM in Phuket, 19–23 July 2009. The HLP is scheduled to meet with the ministers in Phuket on 19 July 2009.

The dilemma facing ASEAN member states as well as the HLP is how to reconcile national political reality with new regional obligation to promote and protect human rights. The ASEAN human rights body is expected to be "realistic", "credible", "workable", "effective", "evolving" and most importantly "acceptable" to all member states. This is easier said than done.

Apart from the caveats in Article 14 mentioned above, we cannot overlook the fact that the ASEAN human rights body will be an organ inside the organizational structure of ASEAN. As such, the ASEAN human rights body is never intended to be a stand-alone independent entity — let alone an autonomous regional watchdog with "sharp teeth".

The HLP is chaired by Ambassador Sihasak Phuangketkeow, Thailand's Permanent Representative to the UN Office in Geneva. He has extensive knowledge of the UN works on human rights, particularly in the Human Rights Council in Geneva. In his opinion, the HLP will have to strike a balance between promotion and protection of human rights when proposing functions for the ASEAN human rights body through the drafting of the terms of reference.

From a more optimistic (and less idealistic) perspective, we can assume that promotion and protection of human rights are closely inter-related. Doing human rights promotion and human rights education will result, more or less, in improving human rights protection in the long run. At the same time, when ASEAN peoples are better informed of their human rights and fundamental freedoms, they would know how to make use of them constructively. In ASEAN, rights and freedoms should always be balanced with duties and responsibilities.

Political diversity in ASEAN makes it unrealistic to try to start human rights cooperation with a "Big Bang". A higher comfort level among member states on human rights cooperation must be developed first. Negotiations on an ASEAN Human Rights Convention will take some time. But basic ground rules and norms for human rights cooperation must be established. After that, more proactive measures can follow, including making country visits to find facts or investigate alleged gross violations of human rights, undertaking periodic peer reviews, and even establishing an ASEAN Human Rights Court to hear cases against member states. This is how human rights cooperation in Europe, Latin America, and Africa has evolved, step-by-step. Nothing is wrong for ASEAN to follow a similar evolutionary path, as long as member states are clearly committed to promoting and protecting human rights through regional cooperation in ASEAN.

In the meantime, efforts in ASEAN to promote and protect rights of women, children, and migrant workers will continue in their own separate processes. A working group has been established to draft the terms of reference for an ASEAN Commission on the Promotion and Protection of the Rights of Women and Children. The cooperation in this area is based on the 2004 Declaration on the Elimination of Violence Against Women in the ASEAN Region, as well as the UN Convention on the Elimination of All Forms of Discrimination Against Women (CEDAW), and the UN Convention on the Rights of the Child (CRC), to which all ASEAN member states have ratified (though Brunei Darussalam, Malaysia, Singapore, and Thailand have different reservations to these UN Conventions).

The ASEAN Committee on the Implementation of the ASEAN Declaration on the Protection and Promotion of Rights of Migrant Workers is working towards the development of an ASEAN legal instrument on the protection and promotion of the rights of migrant workers. This is an important undertaking, because among the ten ASEAN member states, only the Philippines has ratified the International Convention on the Protection of the Rights of All Migrant Workers and Members of Their Families; Cambodia and Indonesia have signed the International Convention but not yet ratified it.

All in all, regardless of what will happen in the HLP and the drafting of the terms of reference for the ASEAN human rights body,[5] ASEAN cooperation on human rights is heading towards the right direction. Cooperation in the functional areas of human rights — protection of the rights of women, children, and migrant workers — is underway. This can be the building block and confidence-building experience among member states, enabling them to engage in and develop cooperation in other (more politically sensitive) areas of human rights through the work of the ASEAN human rights body in the near future.

Building an inclusive and comprehensive ASEAN Community requires patience and long-term planning. Effective promotion and protection of human rights and fundamental freedoms will convince ASEAN peoples to support and participate in the community-building process.

RULES-BASED ASEAN

Becoming a more rules-based organization may mean different things to different member states. At the minimum, it should involve the following:

- Respect for the Charter, adherence to its principles, and prompt application of its provisions;
- Fulfilment of all obligations of the ASEAN membership in accordance with Article 5 Paragraph 2, which includes the enactment of appropriate domestic legislation to effectively implement the Charter provisions and to comply with all obligations of membership;
- Prompt implementation of ASEAN agreements and all other legal instruments;
- Active participation in ASEAN activities with goodwill in cooperation;
- Amicable settlement of disputes arising from the Charter and other ASEAN agreements, including putting in place systematic and efficient dispute settlement mechanisms, and resorting to them when necessary; and
- Compliance with the findings, recommendations or decisions resulting from an ASEAN dispute settlement mechanism, in accordance with Article 27 Paragraphs 1 and 2.

The High Level Legal Experts Group (HLEG), established by the 41st AMM, is looking into details of three issue areas: legal personality of ASEAN; privileges and immunities in ASEAN; and new dispute settlement mechanisms, particularly those that may be required under Article 25 of the Charter. HLEG is also expected to help figure out how to handle "unresolved disputes" which in accordance with Article 26 shall be referred to the ASEAN Summit for its decision.

Becoming more rules-based is a significant departure from the traditional "ASEAN Way" in which flexibility, informality and low-level of institutionalization used to be the norms. From now on, the ASEAN Charter and ASEAN agreements are to be upheld and complied with in both their spirit and letter. Flexibility will have to be limited and uncertainty avoided, especially in the ASEAN Economic Community in which delays and non-compliance would directly hurt the private sector investing in or trading with ASEAN.

Not only new dispute settlement mechanisms will have to be created, but more ASEAN meetings will also have to be convened to ensure speedy decision-making and facilitate prompt implementation. The Charter requires, for example, ASEAN leaders to meet at least twice a year[6] instead of once a year like in the recent past. And the Secretary-General of ASEAN, assisted by the ASEAN Secretariat or any other designated ASEAN body shall monitor the compliance under Article 27.

INSTITUTIONAL BUILD-UP

Apart from the ASEAN human rights body, the Charter also calls for the establishment of the following new mechanisms:

*   ASEAN Coordinating Council (ACC comprising the ASEAN foreign ministers)
*   Three ASEAN Community Councils for each of the Community pillars, and
*   Committee of Permanent Representatives to ASEAN (CPR).

In addition, the Charter calls for the open recruitment of two Deputy Secretaries-General (DSGs) based on merit.[7] The Charter also provides for the appointment of "Ambassador to ASEAN" by non-ASEAN countries, in accordance with Article 46.[8]

With the entry into force of the ASEAN Charter on 15 December 2008, ASEAN has to speed up putting place the necessary new mechanisms in order to operationalize the new institutional framework. The Charter gives ASEAN foreign ministers a few new roles.

NEW ROLES FOR ASEAN FOREIGN MINISTERS

ASEAN Coordinating Council

Article 8.1 of the ASEAN Charter states: "The ASEAN Coordinating Council shall comprise the ASEAN Foreign Ministers and meet at least twice a year." The first two functions of the ACC are to "prepare the meetings of the ASEAN Summit" and to "coordinate the implementation of agreements and decisions of the ASEAN Summit" according to Article 2 (a) and (b). The ACC convened its inaugural meeting on 15 December 2008 when the foreign ministers met at the ASEAN Secretariat to celebrate the entry into force of the Charter on that day.

ASEAN Political-Security Council

The annual ASEAN Ministerial Meeting (AMM) will be renamed as the ASEAN Foreign Ministers Meeting, but the abbreviation AMM will stay. It will come under the ASEAN Political-Security Council (APSC), which will also include the Commission on the Southeast Asia Nuclear Weapon-Free Zone (SEANWFZ Commission), the ASEAN Defence Ministers Meeting, the ASEAN Law Ministers Meeting, the ASEAN Ministerial Meeting on Transnational Crime, and the ASEAN Regional Forum (ARF).

ASEAN Human Rights Body

The AMM shall determine the terms of reference of the ASEAN human rights body. In effect, the AMM will supervise the ASEAN human rights body.

Supervising the Committee of Permanent Representatives to ASEAN

The terms of reference of the Committee of Permanent Representatives to ASEAN was approved at the 41st AMM. After the entry into force of the ASEAN Charter, every member state shall appoint its permanent representative to ASEAN with the rank of Ambassador, who shall be based in Jakarta. Under the ASEAN Charter, the ACC may determine additional functions of the Committee. (The CPR convened its inaugural meeting at the ASEAN Secretariat on 21 May 2009.)

Approve the Appointment of DSGs

The ACC shall approve the appointment and termination of Deputy Secretaries-General (DSGs) upon the recommendation of the Secretary-General (SG). Two of the DSGs shall continue to be nominated by member states, but two others shall be openly recruited. The four DSG posts and the SG post shall be held by nationals of five different ASEAN member states.

Decide on Accreditation of Ambassadors to ASEAN[9]

The AMM shall decide on the accreditation of Ambassadors to ASEAN of non-ASEAN countries and relevant inter-governmental organizations.

First to Consider Amendments to the ASEAN Charter

Proposed amendments to the ASEAN Charter shall be submitted first to the ACC. If there is consensus, the ACC shall then submit them to the ASEAN Summit for its decision, according to Article 48 [2].

Ensure Consistency

Unless otherwise provided for in the Charter, the ACC shall determine the terms of reference and rules of procedure, and shall ensure their consistency, according to Article 49.

FORMATION OF ASEAN COMMUNITY COUNCILS

The formation of the APSC and the AEC Councils is relatively easy: ASEAN foreign ministers and ASEAN economic ministers are most suitable to lead their respective national delegations to meetings of the APSC and the AEC Councils respectively.[10] On the other hand, there is no clear consensus on who shall lead the national delegation to the meeting of the ASCC Council. So far four member states have not made up their minds; hence, the ASCC Council cannot yet convene its inaugural meeting. The AEC Council convened its inaugural meeting on 27 February 2009 in Hua Hin, Thailand. In the meantime, the CPR and the ASEAN Secretariat are formulating standard rules of procedure for use in the three Community Councils.

SINGLE ASEAN CHAIRMANSHIP

Article 31 provides for the single ASEAN chairmanship in each calendar year,[11] based on annual rotation. The member state assuming the chairmanship shall chair: the ASEAN Summit and related summits; the ACC; the three ASEAN Community Councils; the relevant ASEAN Sectoral Ministerial bodies and senior officials; and the Committee of Permanent Representatives. In addition, the ASEAN Defence Ministers Meeting (ADMM), the ASEAN Economic Ministers Meeting(AEM), and the ASEAN Finance Ministers Meeting (AFMM) have agreed to come under the single chairmanship.

NEW FINANCIAL YEAR OF THE
ASEAN SECRETARIAT

In order to synchronize with the new calendar year of the ASEAN chairmanship, the financial year of the ASEAN Secretariat, which used to start on 1 June and end on 31 May, was adjusted to start on 1 January and end on 31 December, starting in 2009.

ASEAN ANTHEM

Article 40 states: "ASEAN shall have an anthem." Thailand had organized a region-wide competition in which a panel of ASEAN representatives, assisted by three independent experts from outside ASEAN, has chosen The ASEAN Way[12] as the winning entry. The ASEAN anthem was played during the celebration of the entry into force of the ASEAN Charter at the ASEAN Secretariat on 15 December 2008.

RESTRUCTURING OF THE ASEAN SECRETARIAT

Apart from recruiting two more DSGs (in addition to the two existing DSGs from nomination by member states on rotation), the ASEAN Secretariat has also undergone a major restructuring to keep up with the new institutional requirements under the Charter. Three new departments have been created to each serve the three community pillars, and the fourth new department handles community affairs (such as legal services, interaction with civil society, public information) and corporate affairs (personnel, administration, and finance).

The ASEAN Secretariat will have to set up a new unit to support the ASEAN human rights body, which is expected to convene its regular meetings at the ASEAN Secretariat. A new Legal Services and Agreements Division has been created under the ASEAN Community and Corporate Affairs Department. This new division requires urgent build-up because the ASEAN Secretariat is now required to provide many new legal services as follows:

1. Interpret the ASEAN Charter

One of the most important new legal tasks to be undertaken by the ASEAN Secretariat is to interpret the ASEAN Charter. Article 51 [1] states: "Upon the request of any Member State, the interpretation of the Charter shall be undertaken by the ASEAN Secretariat in accordance with the rules of procedure determined by the ASEAN Coordinating Council."

The drafters of the ASEAN Charter entrusted this function to the ASEAN Secretariat under the belief that the ASEAN Secretariat is most neutral and objective. And the secretariat staff has the useful institutional memories of what happened during the drafting of the Charter and other ASEAN instruments, knew the deep background of sensitive issues, and understood implicit understanding among member states on certain controversial questions.

2. Support the Chairman of ASEAN or the Secretary-General of ASEAN

Article 23 [2] states: "Parties to the dispute may request the Chairman of ASEAN or the Secretary-General of ASEAN, acting in an ex-officio capacity, to provide good offices, conciliation or mediation." This is new in ASEAN. Probably the ASEAN Secretariat might be called upon to provide necessary support to the Chairman of ASEAN when Article 23 [2] is invoked, and the Chairman was requested to provide good offices, conciliation or mediation. And certainly the Secretariat will have to assist the Secretary-General of ASEAN when he is chosen to provide either one of these DSM services.

3. Support Other DSM

The ASEAN Secretariat will also have to provide necessary support to other DSM, especially the 2004 Enhanced DSM for economic disputes. In this connection, for details of specific roles of the Secretary-General of ASEAN and the ASEAN Secretariat, see the 2004 ASEAN Protocol on Enhanced Dispute Settlement Mechanism.[13]

4. Exercise ASEAN's legal capacities

The ASEAN Secretariat will have to support the Secretary-General of ASEAN and his authorized representatives in exercising ASEAN's legal capacities, both in domestic and international dimensions. One important related task is to negotiate and conclude bilateral agreements with each of ASEAN's dialogue partners[14] on the recognition of ASEAN's legal personality and on P & I for the Secretary-General of ASEAN, his deputies and other ASEAN Secretariat staff as well as officials of member states on ASEAN duty in the territory of each of the dialogue partners.

5. Monitor Compliance and Report to the ASEAN Summit

Article 27 specifies: "The Secretary-General of ASEAN, assisted by the ASEAN Secretariat or any other designated ASEAN body, shall monitor the compliance with the findings, recommendations or decisions resulting from an ASEAN dispute settlement mechanism, and submit a report to the ASEAN Summit."

This obviously is a thankless task, but necessary. For compliance is the essence of being rules-based. Moreover, Article 27 [2] gives right to any member state "affected by non-compliance … [to] refer the matter to the ASEAN Summit for a decision".

6. Safeguard ASEAN's Intellectual Property Rights

The Secretary-General of ASEAN will most probably be entrusted to hold and safeguard ASEAN's intellectual property rights. And he will require support from the ASEAN Secretariat in this regard.

ASEAN's intellectual property includes, for example, the ASEAN Motto: "One Vision, One Identity, One Community" (Article 36); the ASEAN Flag (Article 37); the ASEAN Emblem (Article 38); and the ASEAN Anthem (Article 40); and publications of the ASEAN Secretariat.

7. Monitor Ratification of ASEAN Agreements

The ASEAN Secretariat has to step up its efforts in persuading member states to speed up their respective internal processes in, where required, ratifying ASEAN agreements. In the ASEAN Economic Community, the latest count shows that about 66 per cent of the economic agreements that require ratification have been fully ratified by all member states.

One possible solution to the slow ratification problem is to make new agreements go into effect upon signing. Another solution, which has been in use in some functional agreements (including the 2002 ASEAN Agreement on Transboundary Haze Pollution), is to require ratification of only a majority of member states for an agreement to enter into force in the member states that have ratified it.

8. Ensure Uniformity and Consistency in ASEAN Instruments

The ASEAN Secretariat needs to step in to ensure uniformity, clarity and consistency in the use of proper format and terminology in drafting all ASEAN instruments. One inconsistency that still crops up every now and then is the use of "member countries" instead of "member states" — member states is correct and used in the ASEAN Charter.

9. Ensure Proper Application and Prevent Abuse of Privileges and Immunities in ASEAN

Yet another new legal service that will soon be required to be undertaken by the Secretary-General is to ensure proper application of privileges and immunities under the agreement being drafted by HLEG. The agreement will provide for privileges and immunities to ASEAN, the permanent representatives to ASEAN and their diplomatic staff in the Permanent Missions in Jakarta, officials of member states on ASEAN missions, Secretary-General and the staff of the ASEAN Secretariat, and experts on ASEAN missions, etc. The agreement will require the Secretary-General to help ensure proper application and prevent abuse of the privileges and immunities.

The Charter could be compared to a marriage certificate legally binding its member states to a life-long commitment. Like in a marriage, building the ASEAN Community would require love, caring and sharing, dedication, sacrifice, hard work, and common belief that we are doing the right thing together.

Life in ASEAN after the entry into force of the Charter, especially life at the ASEAN Secretariat, will never be the same again. For there are new hopes, high expectations, and grand vision to live for.

Notes

1. ASEAN certainly did not invent "non-interference". The principle is recognized in the UN Charter and in international law. However, the principle is enshrined in the 1976 Treaty of Amity and Cooperation in Southeast Asia, Article 2b: "the right of every State to lead its national existence free from external interference, subversion or coercion" and Article 2c: "non-interference in the internal affairs of one another" as part of the regional code of inter-state conduct in Southeast Asia.

2. Timor-Leste is keen to join ASEAN by the year 2012. It has set up an ASEAN national secretariat in the Ministry of Foreign Affairs to prepare for the ASEAN membership.

3. The APSC Blueprint, the ASEAN Economic Community (AEC) Blueprint, and the ASEAN Socio-Cultural Community (ASCC) Blueprint are in the Roadmap for an ASEAN Community: 2009–2015. The roadmap also includes the Initiative for ASEAN Integration (IAI) Strategic Framework and IAI Work Plan 2 (2009–2015).

4. *"i. Promote understanding of the principles of democracy among ASEAN youth at schools at an appropriate stage of education, bearing in mind the educational system in the respective ASEAN Member States; ii. Convene seminars, training programmes and other capacity building activities for government officials, think-tanks and relevant civil society organizations to exchange views, sharing experiences and promote democracy and democratic institutions; and iii. Conduct annual research on experiences and lessons learned of democracy aimed at enhancing the adherence to the principles of democracy."*

5. Its official name has not yet been agreed upon. The choices may be narrowed down to two: ASEAN Human Rights Body (because it is already well-known by this name), or ASEAN Human Rights Commission (to give it a more dignified name than just being called a "body").

6. Thailand already hosted the 14th ASEAN Summit in February 2009 in Cha-am/Hua Hin, and will host the 15th ASEAN Summit in October 2009 in Phuket. The "related summits" with dialogue partners in April 2009 that had to be cancelled abruptly because of the violent protests of the "Red Shirts" were to be part of the 14th ASEAN Summit.

7. One of the first DSGs that came through the open recruitment is Mr S. Pushpanathan of Singapore, who is handling the ASEAN Secretariat's coordination with and support for the ASEAN Economic Community. The second DSG from open recruitment will supervise the ASEAN Secretariat's Department of Community and Corporate Affairs. After two rounds of interviews, no one has been found to be most suitable for the job just yet. Third round of interview will soon be underway.

8. So far, all the ten dialogue partner countries and fourteen others have appointed their "Ambassadors to ASEAN"; most of them are concurrently Ambassadors to Indonesia of these countries.

9. Libya's proposed appointment of its Ambassador to ASEAN is being referred to the AMM for consideration.

10. On the AEC Council, Indonesia is represented by the Coordinating Minister for Economic Affairs; all the other nine member states are represented by their ASEAN economic ministers.

11. In the past, the ASEAN chairmanship was handed over to the new chair country at the end of the AMM, which was usually held in July. In order to bridge the gap and adopt the new single chairmanship for one whole calendar year, Thailand assumed the ASEAN chairmanship after the end of the 41st AMM in Singapore in July 2008 and will continue to serve the role until the end of 2009.

12. Music by Kittikhun Sodprasert and Sampao Triudom, lyric by Payom Valaiphatchra, and arrangements by Kittikhun Sodprasert, all from Thailand.

13. Text of the 2004 Protocol is posted on the website of the ASEAN Secretariat, in the Economic Integration section under Dispute Settlement.

14. Australia, Canada, China, the EU, India, Japan, the Republic of Korea, New Zealand, the Russian Federation, the United States, and the UN. Pakistan is ASEAN's sectoral dialogue partner. And Papua New Guinea is a special observer in ASEAN.

SUMMARY OF KEY POINTS

S. Tiwari

This chapter deals with how the Charter had changed or will change ASEAN in four areas.

(a) Impact at National Level of ASEAN Level Democracy

The range of political systems among ASEAN member states extends from the far left (Laos and Vietnam are ruled by

Communist parties) to the far right (Myanmar has a military-led government and Brunei Darussalam is a sultanate), with different types of parliamentary or republican democracies in between. Apart from the United Nations, ASEAN may be the only inter-governmental organization in the world with such political diversity.

Whilst the political system at the domestic level may differ, democracy is very much a part of the ASEAN organization. It remains to be seen how ASEAN regional cooperation will complement national efforts in political development and democratization.

(b) Human Rights: The Dilemma for ASEAN

The human rights body will be known as the "ASEAN Inter-governmental Commission on Human Rights". The name is the result of a compromise to accommodate differing views of ASEAN member states as to whether to use the term "body" or "commission".

Human rights cooperation will be a crucial test for ASEAN. The dilemma that the human rights body will face is how to reconcile national political reality with the new regional obligation to promote and protect human rights. Bearing in mind the political diversity in ASEAN, the progress in relation to human rights is likely to be gradual. The first step will be to develop a higher level of comfort among member states on human rights cooperation.

(c) Rules-based ASEAN

One of the key terms of the Charter is that ASEAN will henceforth be rules-based. What does the term "rules-based" mean? The expression would, at a minimum, involve the following:

- Respect for the Charter, adherence to its principles, and prompt application of its provisions;
- Fulfilment of all obligations of ASEAN membership, including the enactment of appropriate domestic legislation to effectively implement the Charter provisions and to comply with all obligations of membership;
- Prompt implementation of ASEAN agreements and all other legal instruments;
- Active participation in ASEAN activities with goodwill and cooperation;
- Amicable settlement of disputes arising from the Charter and other ASEAN agreements; and
- Compliance with the findings, recommendations or decisions resulting from an ASEAN dispute settlement mechanism.

Becoming rules-based is a significant departure from the traditional "ASEAN Way", in which flexibility, informality and low-level of institutionalization have been the norms. Henceforth the ASEAN Charter and ASEAN agreements need to be upheld and complied with both in letter and spirit. Flexibility will have to be limited and uncertainty avoided, especially in the ASEAN Economic Community, in which delays and non-compliance would directly hurt the private sector investing in or trading with ASEAN.

(d) Institutional Build-up

Apart from the ASEAN human rights body, the Charter provides for the establishment of the following new mechanisms:

- ASEAN Coordinating Council (ACC) comprised of the ASEAN foreign ministers;

- An ASEAN Community Council for each of the three Communities: ASEAN Political-Security Community Council (APSC), ASEAN Economic Community Council (AEC) and ASEAN Socio-Cultural Community Council (ASCC); and
- Committee of Permanent Representatives to ASEAN (CPR).

In addition, there will be four Deputy Secretaries-General (DSGs): two to be selected through open recruitment on the basis of merit and two by nomination by member states in alphabetical rotation. There is also provision under the Charter for the appointment of Ambassador to ASEAN by non-ASEAN countries.

The ASEAN Secretariat has also undergone major restructuring to keep up with the new institutional requirements under the Charter. Three new departments have been created to serve the three community pillars. A fourth new department will handle community affairs (such as legal services, interaction with civil society, public information) and corporate affairs (personal, administration and finance).

4

TRANSLATING THE DESIGN INTO A BLOC
The Domestic Implementation of the ASEAN Charter

Michael Ewing-Chow

INTRODUCTION

The ASEAN Charter[1] was signed on 20 November 2007 at the 13th ASEAN Summit in Singapore and it entered into force on 15 December 2008 on the 30th day after all ten ASEAN member states submitted instruments of ratification to the ASEAN Secretary-General.[2] While the Charter does take the important step of conferring legal personality on ASEAN,[3] it does not completely resolve all the concerns regarding the implementation of the Charter itself.

The implementation problems may arise from three main areas. First, a lack of political will at the state level to implement the treaty. Second, at the domestic level, if the domestic laws are either not in conformity with the treaty or are silent with regard to treaty norms or obligations, the domestic courts applying those laws may not enforce the obligations of the treaty. Finally, there may be administrative structural problems preventing the obligations of the treaty from being applied at the ground level. It is beyond the scope of this chapter to deal with the latter as that will require surveys and interviews at the ground level of each of the ten ASEAN member states for each specific obligation. Instead, it will focus on the former two problems.

In this regard, the terminology used by Brown Weiss and Jacobson regarding strategies for encouraging state compliance with environmental law may be helpful.[4] Using a matrix of "intention" and "capacity", they suggest that a policy toolkit of sanctions, incentives, and "sunshine" can be part of a strategy to strengthen state compliance.[5] Their empirical study showed that where intention and capacity of states to comply were strong, sunshine was the most appropriate tool.[6] Merely highlighting the problem was sufficient as the states usually were able to quickly resolve the issue. However, where capacity was weaker, incentives were necessary to increase the capacity. Highlighting the problem would be insufficient in those cases as the real bottleneck could be the lack of administrative capacity. Conversely, where the state's intention was weaker, then sanctions and sunshine were necessary to encourage compliance.[7] In this situation, international dispute mechanisms were useful to highlight problems and to threaten sanctions so as to encourage political will and "intention".

A. Sanctions

At the international level, as between member states, the Charter does stipulate that where specific ASEAN instruments provide for a dispute settlement mechanism, disputes would be resolved with reference to that mechanism.[8] In particular, disputes concerning the interpretation or application of ASEAN economic agreements would be settled in accordance with the ASEAN Protocol on Enhanced Dispute Settlement Mechanism,[9] which provides for a negative consensus rule[10] for the adoption of any report.[11] While these provisions do provide more certainty for enforcement where there are no pre-existing dispute settlement mechanisms, the Charter suggests that "appropriate dispute settlement mechanisms, including arbitration, shall be established".[12] What those mechanisms will be and how they will be established remains to be seen.

In addition, the Charter also anticipates that if disputes remain unresolved, the dispute shall be referred to the ASEAN Summit for its decision, which will mean that the "ASEAN Way" rule that decisions be made by consultation and consensus will likely be the guiding principle.[13] How this impacts on the right of an ASEAN member to compensation and suspension of concession against another ASEAN member if a measure is not brought into conformity with a dispute settlement report is not entirely clear. The ASEAN Protocol on Enhanced Dispute Settlement Mechanism does provide for such a right, subject to authorization from the Senior Economic Officials Meeting (SEOM).[14] If the SEOM is obliged to continue to make decisions in the "ASEAN Way", while reports may be adopted by negative consensus, the enforcement of such reports will be more problematic.

Nonetheless, ultimately, the Charter is a treaty governed by the 1969 Vienna Convention on the Law of Treaties.[15] While only Cambodia, Malaysia, Myanmar, Philippines and Vietnam are parties to the 1969 Vienna Convention, the 1969 Vienna Convention is generally accepted as codifying customary international law.[16] Thus, regardless of whether they have ratified the 1969 Vienna Convention, the provisions in the treaty that form part of customary international law would apply to ASEAN member states.

Article 26 of the 1969 Vienna Convention provides that "[e]very treaty in force is binding upon the parties to it and must be performed by them in good faith." Article 27 of the 1969 Vienna Convention further provides that "[a] party may not invoke the provisions of its internal law as justification for its failure to perform a treaty."

This is, however, subject to Article 46 of the 1969 Vienna Convention which stipulates that "[a] State may not invoke the fact that its consent to be bound by a treaty has been expressed in violation of a provision of its internal law regarding competence to conclude treaties as invalidating its consent unless that violation was manifest and concerned a rule of its internal law of fundamental importance" and that "[a] violation is manifest if it would be objectively evident to any State conducting itself in the matter in accordance with normal practice and in good faith."

Thus, member states of the Charter are bound by the Charter unless the ratification by any of them was manifestly in violation of a fundamentally important internal law of that member state. To date, no suggestion has been made that this has been the case for any of the ASEAN member states and thus, the Charter is enforceable through the dispute settlement provisions of the Charter. Alternatively, since the Charter is a treaty, disputes could be resolved, perhaps only *in extremis* and with the consent of the parties, by bringing the issue to the International Court of Justice.

B. Sunshine and Incentives

However, what if the problem of implementation was not because of disagreements between the ASEAN member states but caused by internal domestic disagreements in a particular member state or by a lack of legal capacity in that member state to translate the Charter into domestic legislation?

While recourse may be had to international state-to-state dispute resolution, a resolution at the international level may not be sufficient for the domestic courts of that particular member to order the enforcement of the provision of the Charter or the result of the dispute settlement process.[17] It may be necessary then for some "sunshine" to bring the problem to the attention of the ASEAN member states and for ASEAN to look at providing some incentives in the form of capacity-building so as to facilitate the implementation of the obligations. It is hoped that this chapter will bring such "sunshine" to the problem of implementing the Charter at the domestic level and perhaps encourage capacity-building.

THEORIES ON TREATY IMPLEMENTATION

When international law scholars try to categorize how domestic courts have applied international treaties, they usually ask two distinct questions. Some ask whether the domestic law recognizes international treaties without domestic legislation. This question is asked from the perspective of the monist-dualist theoretical dichotomy. Others ask whether the construction of the international treaty itself suggests that it was meant to be applied without such domestic legislation. This is asked by scholars who subscribe to the self-executing treaty theory.

A. Monist-Dualist Dichotomy

In this theoretical dichotomy, there are two theories about the relationship of international law including international treaties like the Charter and the domestic law of member states to the treaties. These two theories are often described as monism and dualism. The differences between the theories, in practice, relate to whether the international treaty has domestic effect, and whether the domestic courts would enforce the treaty.[18]

In a monist legal system, the theory is that international law including treaties and the domestic laws of a member state are assumed to form a unity. Thus, international treaties need not be enacted as domestic legislation for such treaties to have domestic effect and to be upheld by domestic courts. Civil law systems tend towards being monist in their jurisprudence though complexities exist.

In a dualist legal system, the theory is that international law and domestic law do not necessarily form a unity but rather are distinct. Some theorists suggest that this dualism does not create a conflict of laws but rather a conflict of obligations.[19] Regardless, in a dualist legal system international treaties would need to be enacted as domestic legislation before the domestic courts of a member state would apply the provisions found in those treaties.

The common law systems derived from the UK's legal system such as those of Malaysia and Singapore, are generally dualist in nature because the automatic application of treaties signed by the executive would violate the separation of powers — law-making powers being solely the domain of the legislative branch of the government.[20] The position of the other two ASEAN member states which were formerly British colonies, Brunei and Myanmar, is a little more uncertain but they are likely to be dualist as well.

B. Self-executing Treaties

To complicate matters, some legal systems, like that of the U.S., focus less on the dualist-monist question of whether international law and domestic law form a unity but rather, on whether the international treaty in question is self-executing or not. Some have argued that this could be a monist approach as it assumes that a treaty could be self-executing depending on the treaty or the Constitution of the state.[21] However, this does not map completely into the monist-dualist theoretical dichotomy as the reliance on the constitution of a state as the most authoritative document could also suggest a dualist theoretical basis.

Indeed, another theoretical dichotomy arises in this context. Transnationalists, to use Sloss' recent terminology, maintain that the question of whether a treaty is self-executing or not is a question of constitutional law.[22] If the treaty does not encroach on areas in which implementing legislation is required by the Constitution, such as perhaps purporting to appropriate funds,[23] then it is self-executing if the Constitution of that member state provides that treaties shall be part of the law of the member state;[24] conversely, nationalists focus instead on the words of the treaty to see if the treaty "manifests an intention that it shall not become effective as domestic law without the enactment of implementing legislation".[25]

A series of cases[26] on the Visiting Forces Agreement between the Philippines and the United States appears to suggest that the Philippines also adopts the self-executing analysis with the main dispute being whether the United States reciprocally recognized the international agreement as required by the Constitution of the Philippines[27] rather than whether the agreement needed domestic implementing legislation beyond the approval of two-thirds of the Senate of the Philippines.[28] The court in those cases seems to have taken the position that the Visiting Forces Agreement was self-executing. This seems consistent with legal opinion on the application of Convention on the Elimination of All Forms of Discrimination against Women (CEDAW)[29] in the Philippines which suggests that as CEDAW is not self-executing, that it requires implementing legislation.[30] It may well be that as a former colony of the United States, the constitutional jurisprudence of the Philippines has been influenced by the United States.

THE POSITION OF ASEAN MEMBER STATES

These theories tend to be neater in theory than actual practice. Scholars have pointed out that courts have not explicitly referred to these theories in reaching their decisions.[31]

In most domestic court situations, the analysis is done from the perspective of constitutional law rather than international law. Often, however, the Constitution does not specifically provide for implementation processes for treaties and usually only clarifies the relevant authority for the signing and ratification of treaties leaving the domestic courts to develop jurisprudence to fill in the gap.[32] In some cases, pre-existing legislation also allows for administrative procedures to assist the implementation of certain international obligations like that of Executive Certification for State Immunity under the Singapore State Immunity Act.[33]

This chapter will, however, content itself with mapping out the general framework for the implementation of treaties and avoid commenting on the administrative or constitutional law of each individual state.[34] That would be the work of a more massive undertaking.

It is even more complicated in ASEAN where some of the member states' developing legal systems have yet to make definitive pronouncements on the matter.[35] There is a lack of constitutional clarity, judicial decisions and elucidating academic writing about the implementation of treaties in some of the developing countries in ASEAN.

This chapter will, therefore, rely by necessity on the CEDAW State Parties Country Reports for guidance about the implementation of treaties in individual ASEAN member states. All ASEAN member states are also members of CEDAW. Article 18 of CEDAW provides that State Parties must "submit to the Secretary-General of the United Nations, for consideration by the [CEDAW] Committee, a report on the legislative, judicial, administrative or other measures which they have adopted to give effect to the provisions of [CEDAW]". This has resulted in regular CEDAW Country Reports being submitted to the UN explaining how CEDAW has been implemented in each of the CEDAW members. At the moment, these reports provide the best source in the English language for the implementing practices of some of the ASEAN member states.

Cambodia's CEDAW Country Report clarifies that "all the rights as stated in the international human rights covenants are protected by the Constitution of the Kingdom of Cambodia and all principles of the international covenants and conventions take precedence over domestic law"[36] pursuant to Article 31 of the Constitution of Cambodia. While this seems to be limited to human rights treaties, there seems to be an underlying monist assumption as to the implementation of CEDAW without the need for domestic legislation incorporating CEDAW.[37]

Indonesia's CEDAW Country Report suggests that implementing legislation is needed.[38] Laos' CEDAW Country Report states that "due to lack of experience and human resources, the bulk of international treaty obligations has [sic] not been transformed into sustainable and effective national legislative and administrative activities."[39] Malaysia's CEDAW Country Report states that the prohibition on gender discrimination provision in CEDAW needed to be incorporated into the Constitution of Malaysia.[40] Thailand's CEDAW Country Report clarifies that CEDAW cannot be used as a legal instrument in Thailand without domestic legislation.[41] Vietnam's CEDAW Country Report does not clearly state the position though there is an assumption inherent in the report that implementing legislation is needed.[42] All of this suggests a dualist approach to the implementation of treaties for Indonesia, Laos, Malaysia, Thailand and Vietnam.

Singapore's CEDAW Country Report simply states that "Treaties and Conventions do not automatically become part of the law of Singapore unless they are specifically incorporated into the legal system."[43]

Brunei[44] has not yet submitted a CEDAW Country Report as its accession to CEDAW was only on 24 May 2006. The CEDAW Country Reports for Myanmar[45] and the Philippines[46] do not seem to address the issue.

THE ASEAN CHARTER

What does this mean for the Charter?

While much of the Charter governs the relations between ASEAN member states, there are several provisions in the Charter that will likely require clarification as to the process for domestic implementation. Therefore, Article 5.2 of the Charter provides that member states "shall take all necessary measures, including the enactment of appropriate domestic legislation, to effectively implement the provisions of this Charter". Article 5.2 of the Charter, unfortunately, does not resolve the problem of whether Charter is incorporated as part domestic law of a particular member state.

If one adopts the dualist-monist theoretical dichotomy, the fact that the treaty requires all member states to take all necessary measures including the enactment of domestic legislation to implement the treaty does not answer whether the domestic law recognizes the treaty as law without such domestic legislation. If the self executing treaty nationalist perspective is taken, it may be that since the treaty seems to envisage that "appropriate domestic legislation" may be needed, that an argument for its non-self-executing nature may be made though others would argue that Article 5.2 is equivocal at best. Further, the transnationalist would argue that ultimately, regardless of the intention of the treaty, it would depend on the Constitution of each member state.

It is beyond the scope of this chapter to embark on a constitutional analysis of each ASEAN member state or to comment on the jurisprudence of their domestic courts. While such an analysis and commentary will be invaluable as ASEAN integrates and develops, that is a project requiring far more time, resources and local expertise.

Instead, the chapter will content itself with outlining certain provisions in the Charter that may require domestic implementing legislation such as the conferment of legal personality to ASEAN, the requirement to appoint Permanent Representatives to ASEAN and to establish an ASEAN national secretariat, provisions on Immunities and Privileges for ASEAN, ASEAN Permanent Representatives and officials as well as staff of the ASEAN Secretariat, certain fiscal provisions and dispute resolution provisions. At the end of the chapter, some suggestions will be made about how ASEAN may resolve the uncertainty about whether implementing legislation is needed.

A. Legal Personality

Article 3 of the Charter provides for ASEAN to have legal personality. This personality could confer on ASEAN the rights, privileges and immunities of international organizations recognized in international law though much of the details regarding this remains to be clarified.[47]

Legal personality at the domestic level usually means that the entity is granted the capacity to enter into domestic contracts, to sue and be sued and to hold and dispose of properties in its own name. As legal personality is a construct of the state, it is likely that unless a monist approach is taken or the Charter is seen to be self-executing, that some implementing domestic legislation will need to be enacted for ASEAN to have some or all of those elements of domestic legal personality.

Further, even if ASEAN itself is recognized as a juridical entity by the domestic legislation, as ASEAN is quite literally physically "sans teeth, sans eyes, sans taste, sans everything",[48] ASEAN will have to appoint representatives to sign documents and appear in court on its behalf. The recognition of such representatives and how they may be appointed by ASEAN will also need to be clarified by relevant domestic legislation.

Legal personality can also be at the international level. Article 41.7 of the Charter further provides that ASEAN may conclude agreements with countries or sub-regional, regional and international organizations and institutions. The Vienna Convention on the Law of Treaties between States and International Organizations or Between International Organizations 1986[49] does provide for international organizations to enter into binding international treaties, though none of the ASEAN member states are parties to the treaty, and the treaty itself as of 22 June 2009 has yet to enter into force.[50] Regardless, this does not change the fact that should ASEAN enter into an agreement with an ASEAN member state, such an agreement, separate from the authority of ASEAN to enter into an agreement, will have to be subject to the analysis of whether implementing domestic legislation is required.

The status of agreements between ASEAN and entities that are not ASEAN member states is probably more complex as Article 41.7 of the Charter does not clearly specify if such agreements will bind individual ASEAN member states if ASEAN was acting on behalf of those member states. Article 41.7 does however provide that "[t]he procedures for concluding such agreements shall be prescribed by the ASEAN Coordinating Council in consultation with the ASEAN Community Councils."

Going by past practice,[51] all "ASEAN-plus" agreements tend to be signed by the individual member states rather than ASEAN on their behalf. This is so even after the ratification of the ASEAN Charter granting legal personality and the power to conclude agreements to ASEAN.[52]

B. Permanent Representatives and ASEAN National Secretariat

Each ASEAN member state agreed pursuant to Article 12.1 of the Charter to appoint Permanent Representatives to ASEAN with the rank of Ambassador and also agreed pursuant to Article 13 to establish an ASEAN National Secretariat in their home territory. It should be noted that while the Charter does envisage that a committee of Permanent Representatives will be appointed to ASEAN with the rank of Ambassador based in Jakarta,[53] that committee will not be the primary decision-making body. Instead, the ASEAN Summit will continue to be the main forum for decision-making[54] and decisions at all levels will continue to be made by consultation and consensus.[55]

Regardless, as both the appointment of representatives with the rank of Ambassador and the establishment of a domestic ASEAN national secretariat will require an outlay of fiscal expenses, this may require implementing legislation of some sort unless a monist approach is taken.

C. Immunities and Privileges

Beyond the fiscal expenses above, the Charter also provides for immunities and privileges for ASEAN "as are necessary for the fulfilment of its purposes" through separate agreements between ASEAN and the host member state.[56] The Charter further provides for immunities and privileges for the Secretary-General of ASEAN and staff of the ASEAN Secretariat participating in official ASEAN activities or representing ASEAN in the member state "as are necessary for the independent exercise of their functions" which will be spelt out in a separate ASEAN agreement.[57]

While the immunities and privileges are to be spelt out in separate agreements after the Charter, the implementation of those agreements at the domestic level will likely need implementing legislation unless a monist or self-executing treaty doctrine is applied. This is particularly so when dealing with immunity issues as some courts prefer to grant immunity only in clear and unambiguous cases.[58]

Permanent Representatives of the ASEAN member states and officials of the member states participating in official ASEAN activities or representing ASEAN are also to enjoy immunities and privileges "as are necessary for the exercise of their function" and this will be "governed by the 1961 Vienna Convention on Diplomatic Relations or in accordance with national law of the ASEAN Member State concerned".[59] As of 23 June 2009, all the ASEAN member states, with the exception of Brunei, are parties to the 1961 Vienna Convention on Diplomatic Relations.[60] Regardless, like the 1969 Vienna Convention on the Law of Treaties, the 1961 Vienna Convention on Diplomatic Relations is generally seen as codifying the customary international law practice.[61] Even so, the proof of customary international law and proof of the breach of customary international law may be complicated.[62] As such, like before, implementing legislation is probably advisable.

D. Fiscal Provisions

Article 30.1 of the Charter provides that "[t]he ASEAN Secretariat shall be provided with the necessary financial resources to perform its functions effectively" and Article 30.2 of the Charter provides that "the operational budget of the ASEAN Secretariat shall be met by ASEAN Member States through equal annual contributions which shall be remitted in a timely manner."

Under the Charter, the ASEAN Secretary-General and the ASEAN Secretariat have been given greater responsibility to monitor compliance.[63] However, the budget for the ASEAN Secretariat remains very tight. In the financial year 2007/08, the ASEAN Secretariat was given US$9.05 million with each member state contributing equally US$905,000 to the budget.[64] This insistence on equal contributions will likely continue to keep the ASEAN Secretariat budget tight as some of the ASEAN members may find it more difficult to increase their contributions.

The complexity at the domestic level could be added because the Charter does not specifically provide for clear annual contribution rates, preferring instead the ambiguity of "necessary financial resources" for the ASEAN Secretariat "to perform its functions effectively". Thus, it is likely that the annual fiscal contributions for ASEAN will not be set in a treaty but will be probably agreed to administratively at the ASEAN Summit or through some other alternative mechanism. Whether or not a monist, dualist or self-executing treaty perspective is taken, the nature of such an administrative agreement or instrument is even more unclear as they are unlikely to be seen as treaties by themselves. Thus, for such fiscal provisions, perhaps clear fiscal approval processes need to be spelled out to the ASEAN Secretariat by each of the ASEAN member states so that domestic administrative hurdles for the ASEAN Secretariat to receive its budget may be anticipated and avoided.

E. Dispute Settlement

Article 24.1 of the Charter provides that "[d]isputes relating to specific ASEAN instruments shall be settled through the mechanisms and procedures provided for in such instruments" and Article 24.3 of the Charter provides that "[w]here not otherwise specifically provided, disputes which concern the interpretation or application of ASEAN economic agreements shall be settled in accordance with the ASEAN Protocol on Enhanced Dispute Settlement Mechanism."

This of course does not create many problems at the international state to state level. However, if the dispute involves the jurisdiction of a domestic court such as the availability of an investor to state dispute resolution process[65] or a claim against ASEAN by a member state or *vice versa*, the requirement for an "exhaustion of local remedies"[66] may become a barrier against the dispute resolution processes provided in Article 24 of the Charter. Therefore, clear legislative provisions should be provided regardless of whether the Charter is automatically implemented to clarify that in such disputes, there are no local remedies that need exhaustion first before the parties may resort to the dispute settlement mechanisms in the Charter.

F. ASEAN Day

Perhaps the easiest issue regarding the implementation of the Charter is that of the ASEAN Day. Article 39 of the Charter provides that "the 8th of August shall be observed as ASEAN Day." While the Charter does provide for a specific day, perhaps the domestic legislatures or the relevant administrative body delegated with the authority in this regard of each ASEAN member state should spell out the happy terms of how such a day should be celebrated.

CONCLUSION

As this chapter has highlighted, apart from a few clear jurisdictions, the exact process for the implementation of a treaty in many ASEAN member states is still uncertain. Therefore, to be safe, perhaps ASEAN member states should be encouraged to have enacting legislation for most if not all the issues addressed above.

In addition, and alternatively, since more obligations will be created as ASEAN takes further steps to integrate its member states, it is suggested that ASEAN institutes regular monitoring and reporting processes, like those found in Article 18 of CEDAW as elaborated above. This will enable more "sunshine" and perhaps incentives to develop capacity in this area so as to reduce bottlenecks in the implementation of ASEAN treaties.

Nonetheless, while beset with some areas that will need to be addressed as ASEAN evolves, the ASEAN Charter does provide some promise for ASEAN integration. It suggests that there is political will to integrate ASEAN. The question is mainly one of implementation.

Notes

I am grateful to my colleagues, Robert Beckman and Arun Thiruvengadam, for reading earlier drafts of this chapter, providing detailed comments as well as pointing out my mistakes. As always, I still remain entirely responsible for any errors.

1. ASEAN Charter, available at <http://www.aseansec.org/ASEAN-Charter.pdf> (hereinafter "the Charter").
2. ASEAN Charter, Article 47.4.
3. Ibid., Article 3.
4. See Edith Brown Weiss and Harold K. Jacobson, eds., *Engaging Countries: Strengthening Compliance with International Environmental Accords* (Cambridge, MA: MIT Press, 1998), pp. 511–54.
5. Ibid., p. 550.
6. Ibid.
7. Ibid.
8. ASEAN Charter, Article 24.1.
9. Ibid., Article 24.3.
10. Negative consensus means that report is adopted automatically unless there is unanimity against its adoption. The successful claimant usually prevents such unanimity from blocking the adoption of the report.
11. Articles 9.2 and 12.13 of the ASEAN Protocol on Enhanced Dispute Settlement Mechanism, Articles 9.2 and 12.13 available at <http://www.aseansec.org/16754.htm>.
12. ASEAN Charter, Article 25.
13. Ibid., Article 26 read with Article 20.
14. ASEAN Protocol on Enhanced Dispute Settlement Mechanism, Article 16.
15. UNTS 1155, 331, UN Doc. A/CONF.39/11/Add.2 (entered into force 27 January 1980) (hereinafter "1969 Vienna Convention").
16. Anthony Aust, *Modern Treaty Law and Practice* (Cambridge: Cambridge University Press, 2000), pp. 10–11.
17. For a survey of the law and practices of some of the major legal systems on the implementation of treaties, see Thomas Franck and Arun Thiruvengadam, "International Law and Constitution-Making", *Chinese JIL* 2, no. 2 (2003): 467.
18. Simon Tay, "The Singapore Legal System and International Law", in *The Singapore Legal System*, 2nd ed., edited by Kevin Tan (Singapore: Singapore University Press, 1999), p. 471.

19. Gerald Fitzmaurice, "The General Principles of International Law Considered from the Standpoint of the Rule of Law", *Hague Recueil* 92 (1957): 70–80.

20. Lim Chin Leng, "Public International Law Before the Singapore and Malaysian Courts", *SYBIL* 8 (2004): 258.

21. Franck and Thiruvengadam, note 17, p. 472, citing the early U.S. Supreme Court case and still leading precedent of *Foster v Neilson* 27 U.S. (1829): 253.

22. David Sloss, "Schizophrenic Treaty Law", *Texas International Law Journal* 43 (2007): 17–18.

23. See, for example, Article I of the U.S. Constitution which provides that "[n]o money shall be drawn from the Treasury, but in Consequence of Appropriations made by Law."

24. See, for example, Article VI of the U.S. Constitution which provides that "all Treaties made, or which shall be made, under the Authority of the United States, shall be the supreme Law of the Land; and the Judges in every State shall be bound thereby."

25. See Restatement (Third) of the Foreign Relations Law of the U.S. ß 111(4)(a) (1987).

26. See Bayan v. Zamora, G.R. No. 138570, October 10, 2000, Sombilon v. Romulo G.R. No. 175888, February 11, 2009 and Salonga v. Smith G.R. No. 176051, February 11, 2009.

27. Constitution of the Philippines 1987, Section 25, Article XVIII.

28. Constitution of the Philippines 1987, Section 21, Article VII.

29. UNTS 1249, 13 (entered into force 3 September 1981).

30. See Shanthi Dairiam, "The Status of CEDAW Implementation in the ASEAN Countries and Selected Muslim Countries", International Women's Rights Action Watch Asia Pacific, IWRAW Asia Pacific Occasional Papers Series no. 1, available at <http://www.iwraw-ap.org/aboutus/pdf/OPSI.pdf>.

31. Simon Tay, note 18, referring to Rosalyn Higgins, *Problems and Process in International Law* (Oxford: Clarendon Press, 1994), p. 206 and Sloss, note 22.

32. See notes 37–46.

33. State Immunity Act (Cap. 313, 1985, rev. ed., Singapore).

34. Martin Dixon, *Textbook on International Law*, 3rd ed. (London: Oxford University Press, 1996), pp. 87–110.

35. Note 30.

36. UN Doc. CEDAW/C/KHM/1-3, 7.

37. The Constitution of Cambodia (1993) only provides in Article 90 that the Assembly of Cambodia has the power to approve or annul treaties or international conventions.

38. UN Doc. CEDAW/C/IDN/2-3, 7; Constitution of Indonesia (1945) only provides in Article 11 that "[t]he President, with the agreement of the Dewan Perwakilan Rakyat, declares war, makes peace and concludes treaties with other states."

39. UN Doc. CEDAW/C/LAO/1-5, 7; Constitution of Laos (1991) only provides in Article 40 that the National Assembly has the rights and duties "[t]o decide on the ratification or abolition of treaties and agreements signed with foreign countries in accordance with international law and regulations".

40. UN Doc. CEDAW/C/MYS/1-2, 11-12; the Constitution of Malaysia (1957) only provides that the Federal Parliament may only pass laws relating to external affairs including

"Implementation of treaties, agreements and conventions with other countries" as part of the Federal List and may only pass laws on State List issues if it is "for the purposed of implementing any treaty, agreement or convention between the Federation and any other country, or any decision of an international organization of which the Federation is a member".

41. UN Doc. CEDAW/C/THA/2-3, 11; the Constitution of Thailand (2007) only provides in Section 90 that "[a] treaty which provides for a change in the Thai territories or the Thai external territories that Thailand has sovereign right or jurisdiction over such territories under any treaty or an international law or requires the enactment of an Act for its implementation or affects immensely to economic or social security of the country or results in the binding of trade, investment budget of the country significantly must be approved by the National Assembly" and that "[t]here shall be a law determining measure and procedure for the conclusion of a treaty having immense effects to economic or social security of the country or resulting in the binding of trade or investment of the country significantly and the revision or rendering of remedy to the effects of such treaty with due regard to the fairness among the beneficiaries, the affected persons and the general public."

42. UN Doc. CEDAW/C/VNM/2, 11-12; the Constitution of Vietnam (1992 as amended 25 December 2001) only provides in Article 84 that the National Assembly has the power "[t]o decide on fundamental foreign policies, to ratify or nullify international treaties signed directly by the President; to ratify or nullify the signature of or accession to international treaties upon the proposal of the President".

43. UN Doc. CEDAW/C/SGP/1, 22; the Constitution of Singapore (1963, 1999 revised edition) is silent on this matter.

44. The Constitution of Brunei (1959 as revised 1984) is silent about the implementation of treaties.

45. The Constitution of Myanmar (1974) only provides in Article 74 that the Council of State is empowered to "make decisions concerning the entering into, ratification or annulment of international treaties, or the withdrawal from such treaties with the approval of the Pyithu Hluttaw".

46. The Constitution of the Philippines (1987) only provides in Section 21 that "[n]o treaty or international agreement shall be valid and effective unless concurred in by at least two-thirds of all the Members of the Senate."

47. See Simon Chesterman, "Does ASEAN Exist? The Association of Southeast Asian Nations as an International Legal Person", *SYBIL* (2008).

48. William Shakespeare, *As You Like It*, Act II, Scene VII, line 166.

49. UN Doc. A/CONF.129/15 (hereinafter "Vienna Convention 1986").

50. Article 85 of the Vienna Convention 1986 which requires thirty-five state ratifications. As of 22 June 2009, while there are forty parties to the Vienna Convention 1986, only twenty-eight of them are states with the rest being international organizations.

51. See ASEAN-China FTA (ACFTA), ASEAN-Japan Comprehensive Economic Partnership Agreement (AJCEP) and ASEAN Korea (AKFTA), available at <http://www.fta.gov.sg/sg_fta.asp>.

52. See ASEAN-Australia-New Zealand FTA (AANZFTA) signed on 27 February 2009, available at <http://www.fta.gov.sg/fta_aanzfta.asp?hl=41>.
53. ASEAN Charter, Article 12.
54. Ibid., Article 7.
55. Ibid., Article 20.
56. Ibid., Article 17.
57. Ibid., Article 18.
58. Lim, note 20, p. 271, commenting on the Singapore case of *Anthony Woo v. Singapore International Airlines*, 3 *SingLR* 688 (2003).
59. ASEAN Charter, Article 19.
60. UNTS 500, 95 (entered into force 24 April 1964).
61. Lim, note 20, p. 278, citing Eileen Denza, *Diplomatic Law: A Commentary on the Vienna Convention on Diplomatic Relations*, 2nd ed. (New York: Oxford University Press, 1998), pp. 259–60.
62. Lim, ibid., p. 244 referring to the Singapore case of *Public Prosecutor v. Nguyen Tuong Van*, 2 *SingLR* 328 (2004).
63. ASEAN Charter, Articles 11 and 27.
64. ASEAN Secretariat, Media Release, "ASEAN Leaders Sign ASEAN Charter", Singapore, 20 November 2007, available at <http://www.aseansec.org/21085.htm>.
65. See the new ASEAN Comprehensive Investment Agreement, Cha-am, 26 February 2009, available at <http://www.aseansec.org/22218.htm> and the Agreement among the Government of Brunei Darussalam, the Republic of Indonesia, Malaysia, the Republic of the Philippines, the Republic of Singapore and the Kingdom of Thailand for the Promotion and Protection of Investments, Manila, 15 December 1987, available at <http://www.aseansec.org/6464.htm> and the Framework Agreement on the ASEAN Investment Area, Manila, 7 October 1998, available at <http://www.aseansec.org/7994.pdf>.
66. International Law Commission, Draft Articles on Responsibility of States for Internationally Wrongful Acts, with commentaries (2001), UN Doc. A/56/10, *Yearbook of the International Law Commission*, 2001, Vol. II, Part Two, Article 44. Admissibility of claims — The responsibility of a state may not be invoked if: (a) the claim is not brought in accordance with any applicable rule relating to the nationality of claims; (b) the claim is one to which the rule of exhaustion of local remedies applies and any available and effective local remedy has not been exhausted.

SUMMARY OF KEY POINTS

S. Tiwari

This chapter deals with the domestic implementation of the Charter. It examines the problem areas and possible ways of dealing with them.

(a) Implementation Problems: Possible Solutions

Implementation problems may arise in three different ways:

- A lack of political will at the state level to implement the Charter.
- Non-enforcement by the domestic courts of the obligations of the Charter, as the domestic laws are either not in conformity with the Charter or are silent with regard to the Charter norms and obligations.
- Administrative structural problems preventing the obligations of the Charter from being applied at ground level.

Drawing from the analogy of strategies utilized for encouraging state compliance with environmental law, it is suggested that where the intention and capacity of the member states to comply are strong, merely highlighting the problem would be sufficient, as the states are likely to resolve the issue quickly. On the other hand, where capacity was weaker, incentives are necessary to increase the capacity. Conversely, where the member state's intention is weaker, highlighting the problem and sanctions are necessary to encourage compliance.

(b) Provisions Requiring Domestic Implementing Legislation

While much of the Charter governs the relations between ASEAN member states, there are several provisions in the Charter that will require domestic implementing legislation. Some of the more important ones are:

(i) Legal Personality

Legal personality at the domestic level usually means that the entity is granted the capacity to enter into domestic contracts, to sue and be sued and to hold and dispose of property in its own name. Unless a monist approach is taken or the Charter is seen to be self-executing, some implementing domestic legislation will need to be enacted for ASEAN to have some or all of those elements of domestic legal personality.

(ii) Immunities and Privileges

While the immunities and privileges for ASEAN and its officials are to be spelt out in separate agreements after the Charter, the implementation of those agreements at the domestic level is likely to require implementing legislation, unless a self-executing treaty doctrine is applied.

CHARTER IMPLEMENTATION ISSUES AND CONCERNS

S. Tiwari

A brainstorming session on the implementation of the Charter threw up various issues and concerns.

Role of the Permanent Representatives

It was clarified that in view of the appointment of the Permanent Representatives, the role of the ASEAN Directors-General would change. They would handle the coordination work at the national level.

Whose Interests would the ASEAN Human Rights Body Serve?

With the human rights body being inter-governmental and lodged in an inter-governmental structure, it appeared to a participant that the body might end up serving the interests of governments. He proposed that ASEAN sort out the implications of this.

Promotion and Protection of Human Rights

One of the key areas of concern raised in relation to problems of implementation was human rights cooperation. The consensus was that an appropriate manner to reconcile the two aspects of promotion and protection would be to handle the human rights issues arising through gradual means.

Why Secretariat had been Entrusted with the Interpretation of the Charter

It was clarified that the ASEAN Secretariat had been entrusted with the role of interpreting the Charter for the following reasons: one, it was the most neutral body; two, it had the institutional memory of the drafting of the Charter. The work would be performed through a newly setup Legal Services and Agreements Division of the ASEAN Secretariat.

The Focus of Implementation

It was pointed out that dispute settlement was a sensitive area and it would be more profitable for ASEAN to focus on implementation and promotion of compliance with agreements than to emphasize the enforcement aspects. To promote compliance, the Secretariat could also pick up ideas from the models used in other regional organizations. On the other hand, it was pointed out that a strong dispute settlement system was necessary to encourage the promotion of compliance, though there might be no necessity to resort to it.

Protection of ASEAN's Name and Logo

Concern was expressed that non-governmental organizations and businesses were using the ASEAN brand, thus diluting its value. It was agreed that the protection of the name and logo would have to be based on international and domestic rules relating to the protection of intellectual property. ASEAN could also learn from the EU experience in how it protected the EU emblem and name.

5

ASEAN TRADE IN GOODS AGREEMENT (ATIGA)

Kanya Satyani Sasradipoera

BRIEF BACKGROUND AND OBJECTIVE

ASEAN integration in the area of trade in goods had been governed by a number of separate regional legal instruments, such as (i) the Agreement on the Common Effective Preferential Tariffs (CEPT) Scheme for AFTA; (ii) the ASEAN Agreement on Customs (1997); (iii) the ASEAN Framework Agreement on Mutual Recognition Arrangements (1998); (iv) the e-ASEAN Framework Agreement (2000); (v) the ASEAN Framework Agreement for the Integration of Priority Sectors (2004); and (vi) the Agreement to Establish and Implement the ASEAN Single Window (2005). The newly elevated end goal of ASEAN economic integration to establish a single market and production base with free flow of goods by 2015 envisaged in the ASEAN Economic Community (AEC) Blueprint requires ASEAN to adopt a holistic approach by integrating the various existing trade-in-goods related initiatives and adopting new necessary measures into a comprehensive framework. To that end, the ASEAN Economic Ministers (AEM) at their 39th meeting in August 2007 agreed to enhance the CEPT Agreement into a more comprehensive agreement that would set up the disciplines to enable ASEAN to create the necessary environment for the free movement of goods within the ASEAN region. This decision led to the conclusion and signing of the ASEAN Trade in Goods Agreement (ATIGA) by the AEM, which was completed in February 2009.

THE HOLISTIC APPROACH OF THE ATIGA

As mentioned above, the ASEAN Trade in Goods Agreement is the first comprehensive agreement in ASEAN consisting of all necessary provisions to address all aspects related to the flow of goods within the region, ranging from liberalization (tariffs and non-tariffs elimination) to trade facilitation (customs procedures, trade procedures, standards and conformance procedures and sanitary and phytosanitary measures) and trade defence measures. The agreement also encompasses key principles in international trade such as non-discrimination (MFN treatment, national treatment) and transparency. It also consists of provisions on institutional aspects such as dispute settlement, institutional mechanism, review and amendment, and enforcement. The development of the ATIGA was undertaken under the coordination of the Senior Economic Officials Meeting (SEOM) with cooperation and support of other ASEAN Senior Official bodies dealing with goods issues, that is, ASEAN Directors-General of Customs and the Senior Officials Meeting of Agriculture and Forestry (SOM-AMAF).

The ATIGA is not merely a compilation of the various existing agreements and provisions related to trade in goods. A review of the existing agreements and protocols to ensure their relevancy, codification of vague provisions, streamlining of provisions, inclusion of the ministerial decisions to provide legal standing, and last but not least, ensuring synergies of the commitments in various sectors to synergize with other initiatives undertaken in trade in goods were undertaken. With this, the ATIGA was concluded with a far more outreaching coverage as compared to the CEPT Agreement, which was seen as the main agreement in integrating ASEAN trade. It has also made the ATIGA user-friendly to both government officials as the enforcers and the private sector as the beneficiaries, by turning it into a single reference document. The ATIGA's main features as compared to the CEPT Agreement include, among others, the following:

(i) Comprehensive Coverage

The ATIGA covers all areas that are critical in ensuring the realisation of free flow of goods in any regional trading arrangement, that is, tariff liberalization, non-tariff barrier liberalization, rules-of-origin, trade facilitation, customs, standards and conformance, and sanitary and phytosanitary measures. Such comprehensive coverage and the institutional arrangement set up under the ATIGA would also ensure that the various initiatives related to free flow of goods, which are currently being undertaken by various ASEAN sectoral bodies, would be synergized and synchronized to ensure its maximum impact.

(ii) Full Tariff Reduction Schedule

The ATIGA shall annex the full tariff reduction schedule of each member state, which shall spell out the tariff rates applied for each year on each product up to 2015. A single legal enactment by each individual member state to effectively implement the stipulated reduction schedule up to 2015 is also expected. If no single legal enactment can be issued, member states are to issue a legal enactment three months before its effective year. Annexing the full tariff reduction schedules would provide transparency and predictability for the business community and facilitate their strategic planning within the region.

(iii) Non-Tariff Measures

The provisions on non-tariff measures in the ATIGA has been enhanced further through the codification of the relevant provisions and establishment of a mechanism to monitor the application of NTMs with a view to eliminate the non-tariff barriers component of the applied NTMs.

(iv) Trade Facilitation

A dedicated chapter on trade facilitation has been included in the ATIGA to place a much greater emphasis on trade facilitation initiatives with a view to increasing the competitiveness of the region. A comprehensive ASEAN Trade Facilitation Work Programme and an ASEAN Trade Facilitation Framework would also be developed as an integral part of the ATIGA.

(v) Dedicated Sectoral Chapters

A dedicated chapter on each specific area of customs: standards, technical regulations, conformity assessment procedures, and sanitary and phytosanitary measures are included in the ATIGA to provide principle disciplines in these areas that would facilitate the movement of goods. The inclusion of these sectors would enhance coordination among the various initiatives in these sectors and ensure synergy and maximum impact of their respective measures in facilitating trade.

Upon entry into force of the ATIGA, a number of ASEAN economic agreements related to goods, such as the CEPT Agreements and some selected protocols would be superseded by the ATIGA. In case of inconsistency between the ATIGA and any ASEAN economic agreements that are not superseded, the ATIGA shall prevail.

PROGRESS IN THE PREPARATIONS FOR THE ATIGA IMPLEMENTATION

A new committee, the Coordinating Committee on ATIGA (CCA), would be established in accordance with the provisions of Article 90 of the ASEAN Trade in Goods Agreement (ATIGA), to assist the Senior Economic Officials' Meeting (SEOM) and the ASEAN Free Trade Area (AFTA) Council in the performance of their functions in ensuring the effective implementation of the ATIGA. In discharging its function, the CCA would serve as a coordinating and monitoring body on the activities of other working groups, committees and/or sub-committee established under the ATIGA and the progress of implementation in each area covered under the ATIGA. It would also be the body responsible to develop any recommendations to the AFTA Council through SEOM on possible improvements on ATIGA, based on their regular analysis and review on the impact of the ATIGA in ASEAN. The Terms of Reference of this body has been developed for the consideration of the 23rd AFTA Council Meeting in August 2009, Bangkok, Thailand.

A number of main initiatives are now currently being developed based on the provisions under the ATIGA. These include, among others, the following:

(i) Full Tariff Reduction Schedules

Article 19 of the ATIGA requires the finalization of full tariff reduction of member states by the time of entry into force of the agreement for ASEAN-6, and six months after its entry into force for CLMV (Cambodia, Laos, Myanmar and Vietnam). All member states are working on their respective full tariff schedules to be annexed to the ATIGA. The full tariff reduction schedules would be made in AHTN (ASEAN Harmonized Tariff Nomenclature) 2007, and verifications are undertaken to ensure that there are no erosion or back-tracking to the earlier commitments made under CEPT

Agreement or other ASEAN agreement pertaining to tariff liberalization. For the ASEAN-6, it is expected that their full tariff reduction schedules will be endorsed by the 23rd AFTA Council Meeting for subsequent annexing to the ATIGA.

(ii) Elimination of Non-Tariff Barriers

With the tariff elimination nearing to its completion, it is imperative to ensure that the benefits of tariff elimination are not impaired by the adoption of Non-Tariff Barriers embedded in Non-Tariff Measures. The AFTA Council has earlier agreed on the Work Programme on the Elimination of NTBs, which is also included in the Article 42 of the ATIGA, and calls for elimination of NTBs in three tranches with end dates of 2010 for ASEAN-5, 2012 for the Philippines, and 2015/18 for CLMV. However, recognizing that elimination of NTBs should be dealt with in a continuous manner, the article calls for continuous review of NTMs by the various committees under the ATIGA with a view to eliminating the barriers components of the measures and the AFTA Council mandated that the review would be made by "type of measures" approach. A set of disciplines to be observed by ASEAN member states on each type of the non-tariff ensures would be developed to ensure that NTMs to be applied in ASEAN do not have elements that are barriers to trade.

(iii) ASEAN Trade Facilitation Work Programme and Framework

In line with Article 45 of the ATIGA, ASEAN has developed an ASEAN Trade Facilitation Work Programme which sets out all concrete actions and measures with clear targets and timelines of implementation necessary for creating a consistent, transparent, and predictable environment for international trade transactions that increases trading opportunities and helps businesses, including SMEs, to save time and reduce costs. Recognizing the dynamics of global trade arrangements, the work programme was endorsed by the 22nd AFTA Council Meeting in 2008 as a living document. At this juncture, the work programme consists of existing trade facilitation measures undertaken by the various ASEAN sectoral bodies of Trade, Customs, TBT (Technical Barriers to Trade) and SPS (Sanitary and Phytosanitary).

In order to effectively monitor the Trade Facilitation Work Programme, Article 48 of the ATIGA provides for ASEAN member states to individually and collectively assess the implementation of trade facilitation measures set out in the work programme once every two years. For this purpose, the ATIGA calls for the development of an ASEAN Trade Facilitation Framework to serve as a guideline to further enhance trade facilitation in ASEAN. The Trade Facilitation Framework would include a set of questionnaires and a set of common indicators to be adopted by ASEAN and used in undertaking their individual assessment on trade facilitation measures. The ASEAN Work Programme on Trade Facilitation will then be reviewed based on the results of the regular assessment. A pilot project for testing the questionnaire of the framework will be conducted in Indonesia and Vietnam. The outcomes of the pilot project would be reviewed at the 2nd ASEAN Trade Facilitation Joint Consultative Session (JCS) in July 2009 in Singapore and the fine-tuning of the ASEAN Trade Facilitation Framework is expected to be made at the said session prior to submission to the AFTA Council for its endorsement.

In order to effectively implement the ASEAN Trade Facilitation Work Programme and Framework, an ASEAN Trade Facilitation Joint Consultative Committee (ATF-JCC) would also be established. In addition to its role in monitoring the implementation of the work programme and the framework, the ATF-JCC will also serve as a focal point and forum for a dialogue among such national facilitation bodies at the regional level. This forum will strengthen regional cooperation by promoting, coordinating and collaborating policies, recommendations, action plans and the implementation of trade, so that trade transaction costs can be reduced, time efficiency increased, and effective trade control in ASEAN. The draft TOR (terms of reference) of the ATF-JCC is being constructed and will be finalized for consideration and/or endorsement by the 23ʳᵈ AFTA Council Meeting.

(iv) ASEAN Trade Repository

The ATIGA calls for the establishment of an ASEAN Trade Repository (ATR), which is envisioned to be a comprehensive trade repository in ASEAN, serving as a single reference point for all tariff and non-tariff measures applied to good entering, exiting and transiting a country, including all governmental requirements (documentation and procedures) regarding a specific commodity. Options of the ATR concept and the policy issues in each option in order to develop the appropriate design and steps to be taken in establishing the ATR are currently being deliberated at the Coordinating Committee for the Implementation of CEPT AFTA (CCCA).

In conclusion, the enforcement of the ATIGA is in line with the process towards realizing the ASEAN Economic Community by 2015 and its key features would enhance transparency, certainty and predictability in the ASEAN legal framework and enhance the ASEAN rules-based system. With this, it is expected that the ATIGA would also enhance confidence of the business community as well as foreign investors, and the attractiveness of ASEAN as an investment destination compared to other region such China and India.

SUMMARY OF KEY POINTS

S. Tiwari

(a) The Trade in Goods Area — Need for a Holistic Approach

ASEAN has had various instruments related to trade in goods: (i) the Agreement on the Common Effective Preferential Tariff (CEPT) Scheme for the ASEAN Free Trade Area (AFTA, 1992); (ii) the ASEAN Agreement on Customs (1997); (iii) the ASEAN Framework Agreement on Mutual Recognition Arrangements (1998); (iv) the e-ASEAN Framework Agreement (2000); (v) the ASEAN Framework Agreement for the Integration of Priority Sectors (2004); and (vi) the Agreement to Establish and Implement the ASEAN Single Window (2005). The newly elevated end-goal of ASEAN economic integration to establish a single market and production base with free flow of goods by 2015 envisaged in the ASEAN Economic Community (AEC) Blueprint requires ASEAN to adopt a holistic approach by integrating the various trade-in-goods related initiatives and adopting new measures into a comprehensive framework. Further, some of the instruments have existed for a long time and need to be reviewed and updated. The end result is the enhancement of the CEPT Agreement into a more comprehensive agreement that would set up the disciplines to enable ASEAN to create the necessary environment for the free movement of goods within the ASEAN region.

(b) Enhancing Business Confidence

An outcome of the exercise to review, improve and enhance so as to move towards realizing the ASEAN Economic Community by 2015, is the ASEAN Trade in Goods Agreement

(ATIGA) — the first comprehensive agreement in ASEAN consisting of the necessary provisions to address all aspects related to the flow of goods within the region, ranging from liberalization (tariff and non-tariff elimination) to trade facilitation (customs procedures, trade procedures, standards and conformance procedures and sanitary and phytosanitary measures) and trade defence measures. The agreement also encompasses key principles in international trade (such as non-discrimination, most-favoured-nation treatment, national treatment) and transparency. It further covers provisions on institutional aspects.

The ATIGA is not merely a compilation of the various existing agreements and provisions related to trade in goods. In finalizing the ATIGA, a review of the existing agreements and protocols to ensure their relevancy, clarification of vague provisions, streamlining of provisions, inclusion of ministerial decisions to provide legal standing, and finally synergies of the commitments in various sectors were also undertaken. Accordingly, the ATIGA has a more comprehensive coverage than the CEPT Agreement, which was seen as the main agreement in integrating ASEAN trade. Further, the ATIGA is user-friendly to both government officials as the enforcers and the private sector as the beneficiaries, as it is a single reference document.

(c) The New Features in the ATIGA

The new features of the ATIGA, as compared with the CEPT Agreement, include, among others, the following:

- **Coverage**. The ATIGA covers all areas that are critical in ensuring the realisation of the free flow of goods in a regional trading arrangement,
- **Full Tariff Reduction Schedule**. The ATIGA has consolidated the full tariff reduction schedule of each ASEAN member state, which had been scattered in various places under the

CEPT. It will spell out the tariff rates applied for each year on each product up to 2015. Annexing the full tariff reduction schedule to the ATIGA would provide transparency and predictability for the business community and facilitate strategic planning within the region.

- **Non-Tariff Measures (NTM)**. The provisions on non-tariff measures in the ATIGA have been enhanced through an expanded codification of the relevant provisions and the establishment of a mechanism to monitor the application of NTMs.
- **Trade Facilitation**. There is greater emphasis on trade facilitation initiatives under the ATIGA.

(d) ASEAN Trade Repository

The ATIGA provides for the establishment of the ASEAN Trade Repository (ATR). The ATR is another new initiative to enhance transparency in ASEAN. It is envisioned to be a comprehensive trade repository, serving as a single reference point for all tariff and non-tariff measures applied to goods entering, exiting and transiting a country, including all governmental requirements (documentation and procedures) regarding a specific commodity. Options of the ATR concept and the policy issues in each option in order to develop the appropriate design and steps to be taken in establishing the ATR are currently being deliberated.

(e) Initiatives under ATIGA

A number of initiatives are being developed based on the provisions of the ATIGA. These include: (i) full tariff reduction schedules; (ii) a set of disciplines to be observed by ASEAN member states on each type of non-tariff measure to ensure that NTMs to be applied in ASEAN do not have elements that are barriers to trade; (iii) ASEAN Trade Facilitation Work Programme and Framework.

6

THE ASEAN COMPREHENSIVE INVESTMENT AGREEMENT 2009
Its Objectives, Plan and Progress

Yap Lai Peng

BACKGROUND

Since the Asian financial crisis in 1997/98, ASEAN has been working towards building up its economic resilience to external shocks by reinforcing macroeconomic fundamentals at the national levels and seeking to strengthen global and regional integration. ASEAN's intention is to transform itself into a regional powerhouse that would be a driver of both regional and global expansion through regional integration. The 1997 ASEAN Leaders' Declaration agreed on the transformation of ASEAN into a stable, prosperous and highly competitive region (ASEAN Vision 2020). At its 2003 meeting in Bali, ASEAN Leaders declared that the ASEAN Economic Community (AEC) shall be the goal of regional economic integration by 2020 (Bali Concord II) and this goal was accelerated to 2015 at the Cebu Summit in 2007.

In making the AEC a reality, ASEAN intensified internal integration measures towards the process of evolving into an economic area that would take advantage of the strong economic potential of a combined market of close to 600 million people. The ASEAN Economic Community Blueprint (AEC Blueprint) was developed as a single and coherent roadmap for advancing the AEC by identifying the characteristics and elements of the AEC, with clear targets and timelines.

Under the Blueprint, legal instruments of regional integration were reviewed to make them relevant to the present competitive global economic environment. These measures included the review of the various goods agreements and protocols and their integration into a single comprehensive agreement known as the ASEAN Trade in Goods Agreement (ATIGA). In addition, the ASEAN Investment Area (AIA) Council of Ministers agreed to step up regional efforts in attracting FDI. In 2007, the AIA Council agreed to revise the 1987 Agreement for the Promotion and Protection of Investments (known as the Investment Guarantee Agreement or "ASEAN IGA"), and the 1998 Framework Agreement on the ASEAN Investment Area (AIA) or the "AIA Agreement", as well as its two related protocols, into a single agreement to be known as the *ASEAN Comprehensive Investment Agreement* (ACIA). The ACIA was concluded in 2008 and signed in 2009.

OBJECTIVES OF ACIA

The ACIA was envisioned with the view of revising and merging the AIA and IGA agreements into a single comprehensive ASEAN investment agreement. Given the competitive global environment for foreign direct investment, the ACIA was to be drafted with the aim of creating a freer and more open investment regime towards the achievement of ASEAN economic integration, based on international best practices. ACIA would facilitate the transformation of ASEAN into an investment hub that would be able to compete effectively with other emerging economies.

In particular, the objectives of the ACIA are:

i.   Progressive liberalization of the investment regimes of member
       states;
ii.   Provision of enhanced protection to investors of all member
       states and their investments;
iii.   Improvement in transparency and predictability of investment
       rules, regulations and procedures conducive to increased
       investment among member states;
iv.   Joint promotion of the region as an integrated investment
       area; and
v.   Cooperation to create favourable conditions for investment by
       investors of a member state in the territory of the other member
       states.

The ACIA was drafted based on the following guiding principles:

i.   Provide for investment liberalization, protection, investment
       promotion and facilitation;
ii.   Progressive liberalization of investment with a view towards
       achieving a free and open investment environment in the
       region;
iii.   Benefit investors and their investments based in ASEAN;
iv.   Maintain and accord preferential treatment among member
       states;
v.   No back-tracking of commitments made under the AIA
       Agreement and the ASEAN IGA;
vi.   Grant special and differential treatment and other flexibilities
       to member states depending on their level of development
       and sectoral sensitivities;
vii.   Reciprocal treatment in the enjoyment of concessions among
       member states, where appropriate; and
viii. Accommodate expansion of scope of this agreement to cover
       other sectors in the future.

The key features of the ACIA are:

- Comprehensive investment liberalization and protection provisions
- Clear timelines for investment liberalization in line with the ASEAN Economic Community;
- Benefits extended to foreign-owned ASEAN-based investors;
- Preservation of AIA preferential treatment; and
- A more liberal, facilitative, transparent and competitive investment environment.

ACIA vs. AIA

The ACIA is intentionally drafted to provide a better investment environment for ASEAN-based investors and investments. The key differences between the ACIA and the AIA are manifold. Foremost is that the ACIA is a single investment agreement, containing more comprehensive provisions, covering the four pillars of investment: liberalization, protection, facilitation and promotion. It provides for the clear interaction of the various provisions of liberalization and protection whereas the AIA and the ASEAN IGA were two separate agreements with no clear interface between the liberalization and the protection provisions.

Of note is that ACIA grants immediate benefits to ASEAN investors and ASEAN-based foreign investors, with the deadline to achieve free and open investment shortened to 2015. In contrast, the AIA confers benefits on ASEAN investors first, that is, national treatment shall be extended to ASEAN investors by 2010, while for non-ASEAN investors, national treatment is only extended in 2020.

The scope of the ACIA, while similar to that of the AIA, namely covering manufacturing, agriculture, fishery, forestry, mining and quarrying, and services incidental to manufacturing, agriculture, fishery, forestry, mining and quarrying, has been expanded to cover portfolio investments and could also accommodate any other sectors in the future, as may be agreed upon by all member states. In addition, while the ACIA like the AIA, does not cover the services sectors other than services incidental to the five sectors, the protection elements of ACIA have been extended to any measure affecting the supply of a service by a service supplier of a member state through commercial presence in the territory of any other member state, to the extent that they relate to an investment and obligation under this agreement and regardless of whether or not such service sector is scheduled in the member states' schedule of commitments made under the ASEAN Framework Agreement on Services (AFAS).

The ACIA also provides for comprehensive definitions in line with international investment agreements, while the AIA had limited definitions and investment was not defined under the AIA. In addition, the ACIA contains procedures for the modification of schedules of commitments with compensatory adjustment, but such procedures were not provided for under the AIA where modifications are presented only to the AIA Council, which was the arbiter.

Of note is the difference in approach towards scheduling of reservations under the ACIA. The AIA adopted a two-track approach of the Temporary Exclusion List (which was to be phased out by 2010/2015) and the Sensitive List (in which certain sectors remain closed to both ASEAN and non-ASEAN investment but is subject to a review, with the possibility of elimination from the list or a transfer to the TEL). Under the ACIA, ASEAN adopts a single list approach of scheduling reservations. This is also a major departure from the approaches adopted under other ASEAN FTAs (AKFTA [ASEAN-Korea Free Trade Agreement], AANZ [Agreement Establishing the ASEAN-Australia-New Zealand Free Trade Area] — two-list approach). The ACIA reservations will only be taken in respect of national treatment and senior management and board of directors (SMBD), whereas the AIA provides for limitations in respect of whether the sectors are closed for foreign participation without clear specifications on what types of limitations that can be imposed. The ACIA also prohibits the use of TRIMS performance requirements and there is provision for a review to include the need for additional commitments. As a consequence, the liberalization elements of the ACIA are far wider in scope than the AIA.

In addition to the state-to-state dispute settlement under the ASEAN Protocol on Enhanced Dispute Settlement Mechanism, the ACIA has a dedicated section with detailed provisions on Investor-to-State Dispute Settlement (ISDS) between an investor and a member state. The ISDS provisions are more comprehensive, including detailed arbitration procedures. In addition, under ACIA, the disputing investor is given the right to choose the arbitration institution where before it was the joint decision of the disputing parties. There is also a new article on consultations among member states on ACIA matters and its implementation.

BENEFITS OF ACIA

The *raison d'être* of the ACIA is to provide a better investment environment with more predictable and transparent rules. The improved investment environment includes the following:

- The achievement of free and open investment regime by 2015 when member states are ready to reduce or eliminate investment impediments (reservation lists) according to the three strategic schedules of the AEC.
- ACIA's comprehensive provisions will enhance protection of investment and improve investors' confidence to invest in ASEAN.
- It encourages further development of intra-ASEAN investments, especially among MNCs based in ASEAN through expansion, industrial complementation and specialization.
- It enhances economic integration.

For the business sector, ACIA will also bring benefits, among which are:

- ASEAN-based investors can enjoy the benefits of non-discriminatory treatment when they invest in other ASEAN countries. They will be granted similar treatment as domestic (host country) investors, and also similar treatment *vis-à-vis* other ASEAN-based investors (subject to the reservations).
- In cases of disputes with host governments, investors have a choice to bring a claim in domestic courts (where applicable), or international arbitration.
- Investors and their investments will be granted fair and equitable treatment and full protection and security.
- Assurance of free transfer of funds, including capital, profits, dividends, etc.
- Investments will not be expropriated, except for public purposes. Clear provisions on compensation based on fair market value.
- Non-discriminatory treatment for compensation for losses arising from civil strife, riots, etc.
- Cooperation from ASEAN governments in terms of promotion and facilitation of investment.

PLAN AND PROGRESS OF THE ACIA

The ACIA was signed in February 2009. Under the terms of the agreement, the ACIA shall enter into force after all member states have notified or, where necessary, deposited instruments of ratification with the Secretary-General of ASEAN.

Member states are in the process of undergoing domestic procedures for the ACIA to enter into force. The aim is to complete these procedures as soon as possible. In parallel with these domestic procedures, member states also have the task of preparing the reservation lists to be annexed to the agreement. The Coordinating

Committee on Investment has charge of reviewing these lists which are expected to be forwarded to the AIA Council for its endorsement.

SUMMARY OF KEY POINTS

S. Tiwari

Under the ASEAN Economic Community Blueprint, the review of the instruments of regional integration to make them relevant to the competitive global economic environment included the revision of the 1987 Agreement for the Promotion and Protection of Investments (known as the Investment Guarantee Agreement or "ASEAN IGA") and the 1998 Framework Agreement on the ASEAN Investment Area (AIA) or the "AIA Agreement" and their consolidation into a single agreement to be known as the ASEAN Comprehensive Investment Agreement (ACIA). The ACIA was concluded in 2008 and signed in February 2009.

Given the competitive global environment for foreign direct investment, the ACIA has been drafted with the objective of creating a freer and more open investment regime towards the achievement of ASEAN economic integration on the basis of international best practices. It is hoped that the ACIA would facilitate the transformation of ASEAN into an investment hub that would be able to compete effectively with other emerging economies.

(a) What is New in the ACIA?

The ACIA is a single investment agreement containing more comprehensive provisions and covering the four pillars of investment: liberalization, protection, facilitation and promotion. Of note is that the ACIA grants immediate benefits to ASEAN investors and ASEAN-based foreign investors, with the deadline to achieve free and open investment shortened to 2015.

The scope of the ACIA has been expanded to cover portfolio investments and could also accommodate any other sectors in the future that may be agreed upon by all member states. In addition to the five listed sectors, the protection elements of the ACIA have been extended to any measure affecting the supply of a service by a service supplier of an ASEAN member state through commercial presence in the territory of any other member state, to the extent that they relate to an investment and obligation under the ACIA and regardless of whether or not such service sector is included in the member states' schedule of commitments made under the AFAS.

The ACIA also provides for comprehensive definitions in line with international investment agreements.The AIA had limited definitions and investment was not defined in it. In addition, the ACIA contains procedures for the modification of schedules of commitments with compensatory adjustment.

In addition to the state-to-state dispute settlement under the ASEAN Protocol on Enhanced Dispute Settlement Mechanism, the ACIA has a dedicated section with detailed provisions on investment disputes between an investor and an ASEAN member state. The investor-state dispute settlement provisions are more comprehensive under the ACIA. Further, the disputing investor is given the right to choose the arbitration institution; before the ACIA, it was based on the joint decision of the disputing parties.

(b) Benefits of ACIA for the Business Sector

Some of the possible benefits which the ACIA will bring to the business sector are:

- ASEAN-based investors can enjoy the benefits of non-discriminatory treatment when they invest in other ASEAN countries. They will be granted similar treatment as domestic (host country) investors, and also similar treatment (subject to the reservations) *vis-à-vis* other ASEAN-based investors;
- In cases of disputes with host governments, investors have a choice to bring a claim in domestic courts (where applicable) or utilize international arbitration;
- Investments will not be expropriated, except for public purposes; there are clear provisions on compensation based on fair market value;
- Cooperation from ASEAN governments in terms of promotion and facilitation of investments.

The ACIA was signed in February 2009. It will enter into force after all member states have notified or, where necessary, deposited instruments of ratification with the Secretary-General of ASEAN.

PRIVATE SECTOR PERSPECTIVES

7

THE ASEAN CHARTER AND THE ASEAN ECONOMIC COMMUNITY
A Watershed for Regional Economic Integration?

Razeen Sally

ASEAN is armed with a new "charter". The ASEAN Charter gives the group a common legal personality; it contains (minor) institutional innovations; and it houses an ASEAN Political-Security Community, an ASEAN Sociocultural Community and, not least, the pre-existing ASEAN Economic Community (AEC). On the economic front, the Charter contains two new agreements, the ASEAN Trade in Goods Agreement (ATIGA) and the ASEAN Comprehensive Investment Agreement (ACIA). These integrate separate agreements into single consolidated legal texts on trade in goods and foreign direct investment respectively. The ASEAN Framework Agreement on Services (AFAS) remains unchanged.

What are we to make of the new-look ASEAN? Outsiders have long belittled ASEAN for its internal divisions and lack of integration. ASEAN rhetoricians counter that with its brand-new

Charter, its AEC Blueprint, and indeed its new free trade agreements (FTAs), ASEAN has reached a watershed. In future it will spur intra-regional integration, be a viable collective force in wider Asian and international relations, and collectively counter common challenges — not least the present global economic crisis.

I remain a sceptical outsider. My preference is to take a cool, hard look at the ASEAN economic track record and the real forces driving regional economic integration. I do not take ASEAN rhetoric at face value, nor do I confine myself to legal micro-details. The job of the economist, especially one with a strong applied interest in policies and institutions, is to survey the forest, not to rhapsodize its sylvan beauty, nor to microscopically examine its trees in splendid isolation.

Do not get me wrong. ASEAN is better than nothing. It is good for politicians and officials to meet regularly and jaw-jaw. In a region historically riven by conflict and violence, that is better than the alternative. If member governments can agree on modest common denominators, so much the better. Beyond serving as a marginally useful chat forum, does ASEAN, as an economic entity, have substance? Will the Charter and the AEC make a difference? Let's start with the ASEAN track record, and then move on to the Charter.

THE ASEAN TRACK RECORD

ASEAN's economic core is the ASEAN Free Trade Area (AFTA). Its vaunted success is the Common Effective Preferential Tariff (CEPT). Intra-regional tariffs have come down close to zero in the old ASEAN members, with longer transition periods for the poorer new ASEAN members. But the CEPT is mostly a paper exercise: ASEAN countries' tariffs have been coming down unilaterally in any case; and there has been minimal take-up of CEPT preferences by firms. ASEAN also has agreements on tackling non-tariff barriers and liberalizing services and investment, but these are very weak and have resulted in hardly any net liberalization. In sum, ASEAN economic integration has been limited to tariff cuts, but it has a pathetic record in tackling intra-regional regulatory barriers. The latter, more than the former, impede regional economic integration — for MNEs with their cross-border manufacturing supply chains, for home-based firms, for agricultural and services suppliers, and for final consumers.

Given this context, there will be no true AEC — an integrated market for goods, services, investment and skilled labour — by 2015. Regional integration is pretty much limited to MNE supply chains in slices of global manufacturing, overwhelmingly in ICT products. Beyond that, ASEAN has no "single market" in the European sense or even in the North American sense (that is, regional production for regional consumption). Given ASEAN's track record, it has no prospect of coming close to a single market by 2015, 2020 or even 2025. To talk EU-style single market language is risible. It is also way off-track to talk of emulating the "EU model" in terms of building common institutions and strengthening common policies. The EU model is almost totally irrelevant to ASEAN. Political, economic, cultural and institutional gaps in Southeast Asia are historically larger than they are in Europe; and there is precious little of a common tradition, cultural and otherwise, to draw on for anything more than quite shallow integration. Much of the surreal chatter about emulating the EU model comes from Brussels.

What about ASEAN FTAs with third countries? ASEAN now has FTAs on the books with Japan, South Korea, China and Australia-New Zealand. It seems close to concluding one with India and is negotiating with the EU. Again, one should distinguish hype from reality. The reality is that these FTAs are weak to very weak. The FTA with Australia-New Zealand is at the less-weak end of the spectrum; the almost-concluded FTA with India is at the other, very weak end of the spectrum. The strongest of them take 90 per cent of tariff lines or trade volumes down to zero (more or less), but make very little dent into non-tariff regulatory barriers. They are advertised as WTO-plus, which in some cases is literally true. But that means little in practice, for WTO disciplines on export restrictions, services, investment, government procurement and a host of other regulatory barriers are also weak to very weak. In short, with few exceptions, ASEAN FTA provisions are not strong enough to change existing national practice in a liberalizing or trade facilitating direction. Besides, they are complicated by differing rules-of-origin requirements, and by the bilateral FTAs individual ASEAN members have with third countries. All the above is an external reflection of the limits of intra-ASEAN economic integration.

No wonder then that U.S. "deep-integration" FTAs with Thailand and Malaysia got stuck in a quagmire. No wonder there is no serious prospect of a U.S.-ASEAN FTA. And no wonder the EU-ASEAN FTA negotiations have been stuck from the start. ASEAN collectively, and indeed ASEAN countries individually except Singapore, are simply not serious about FTAs. Intra-ASEAN divisions have proved intractable; and ASEAN lacks a credible common negotiating machinery.

The bald reality is that trade and FDI liberalization, and with it *partial* regional integration through MNE supply chains, have *not* come about "top-down" as a result of ASEAN initiatives. Rather, what exists of regional integration is the product of *unilateral* measures by individual ASEAN countries, progressively emulated by other ASEAN countries. Such unilateral liberalization of trade and FDI has itself been partial and patchy, mainly bunched in manufacturing sectors. It has been more limited in agriculture and services, which goes far to explain the lack of regional integration in these sectors.

But unilateral liberalization has stalled in the region since the Asian crisis, which reflects a global trend. It has stalled in Malaysia, Thailand, Indonesia and the Philippines. Malaysia and Thailand have internal political instability and are treading water on the economic front. Thailand's political and economic blockages have caused uncertainty among foreign investors, not least due to unpredictable changes in FDI regulations. Indonesia and the Philippines have seen creeping protectionism in some sensitive sectors, particularly in agriculture. All four have not seen significant domestic pro-competitive structural reforms, as the World Bank's annual Doing Business indicators illustrate. The main exceptions to this pattern are Singapore and Vietnam. Singapore accelerated unilateral liberalization in services in response to the Asian crisis. And Vietnam accelerated its external liberalization and structural reforms in the run-up to its WTO accession in 2007.

What has happened since the outbreak of the global economic crisis? The global trend is that a sharp contraction in growth, and even sharper contractions in international trade and FDI (the "deglobalization" phenomenon), have not led to a quantum leap in protectionism. Indeed, new trade-restrictive measures have been remarkably restrained. Increases in tariffs and basic non-tariff barriers have been limited to a small number of countries and bunched in a few sectors. More worrying, however, is the creeping increase in non-tariff, regulatory barriers such as discriminatory subsidies, foreign investment restrictions, discriminatory government procurement, and more arbitrary application of technical and food safety standards.

This is also the pattern in Southeast Asia. Mixed signals have come from the region. On the one hand, Vietnam and Indonesia have increased trade restrictive measures. Indonesia stands out with a range of import tariff hikes, new import licensing measures, government procurement restrictions and tighter application of standards (such as pre-shipment inspection) to imports. On the other hand, Malaysia recently announced major liberalization of FDI in services sectors, in response to domestic political circumstances and anaemic inward investment. But overall, ASEAN collectively has done nothing to stem emerging protectionism in the wake of the crisis, despite pledges to do so. That is in keeping with past performance and is perfectly predictable. As usual, it has been left to individual member states to respond in their different ways.

Given this context, it is pie-in-the-sky to expect a stronger ASEAN while underlying weaknesses and divisions among its member-states persist or even get worse. Hence any attempt at top-down ASEAN integration is thoroughly misguided, indeed utopian.

THE ASEAN CHARTER

Now turn to the ASEAN Charter. Is it more than a paper tiger? It is big on principles and ambitions. Its language is lofty. It codifies existing norms. But what about substance? Let's take a look at the new agreements on trade in goods and FDI, ATIGA and ACIA.

The ATIGA brings together a range of regional instruments: AFTA's CEPT, and ASEAN agreements on customs, mutual recognition arrangements, e-commerce, priority sectors and a single window (for customs clearance of goods). It codifies existing provisions on tariffs, NTBs, trade facilitation and other trade-related measures. But, at face value, that is almost all it seems to do.

As mentioned before, NTBs and regulatory barriers are the core obstacles to market access within ASEAN. For example, ASEAN's existing deadlines to eliminate NTBs will probably not be met, partly because it is up to member governments to table their own NTBs for elimination, and partly due to poor implementation. Also, even some old ASEAN members are not on target to introduce national single windows for customs clearance. The ATIGA does not appear to contain new initiatives or legal instruments to tackle NTBs. So what is really new about it?

The ATIGA's one small innovation is its call for the establishment of an ASEAN Trade Repository (ATR). This is supposed to be a comprehensive database and a single reference point for all tariff and non-tariff measures on cross-border trade in the region. That is a good idea. If designed and implemented properly, it could inject much needed transparency into trade policies in ASEAN. But that is a big "if".

The ACIA is more interesting. In addition to bringing together a range of FDI instruments in different legal texts, the potential advantages of ACIA are: the extension of national treatment to ASEAN-based foreign investors from the start, with a shorter deadline for full liberalization (2015); wider scope of investments covered; a single negative list for scheduling reservations; and a new investor-to-state dispute settlement mechanism to complement existing ASEAN state-to-state dispute settlement.

Potentially, these novelties could strengthen investment liberalization and investor protection compared with the old ASEAN Investment Area (AIA). But it leaves big questions and gaps. And it all depends on how provisions are fleshed out, interpreted and implemented. What will be the criteria for ASEAN-based MNEs to qualify for non-discriminatory treatment? How will investments covered by ACIA relate to services covered by AFAS, especially through "commercial presence" (that is, FDI through "mode three of supply" in WTO jargon)? Bear in mind that the AFAS, a weak agreement that is barely stronger than the WTO's very weak General Agreement on Trade in Services (GATS), remains unchanged. Will disciplines cover both pre- and post-establishment regulatory barriers? "Post-establishment" regulatory barriers, for example, licensing and operating requirements for foreign service-providers, are the biggest obstacles to trade in services; and they are also the most difficult to discipline through multilateral, bilateral and regional agreements. How will governments use (or abuse) the single negative list? Finally, what shape will investor-to-state dispute settlement take? If it turns out to be more than a paper tiger, it could have unanticipated and surprising consequences for ASEAN member governments.

In general, I do not hold out much hope for these new agreements to be a vehicle for trade and FDI liberalization in ASEAN. That is too much to ask of the ASEAN Charter. If the Charter is to have additional value, I think it lies in the modest goal of improving transparency rather than out-of-reach ambitions to directly accelerate liberalization and regional integration.

All ASEAN members — even to some extent Singapore — have more-or-less opaque trade policies. There is a lack of publicly available information on swathes of trade and FDI regulations, especially of the non-tariff, behind-the-border variety. Also lacking is systematic assessment of the costs and benefits of different policies and communication of findings to the public. More transparency in all these respects would facilitate more informed discussion about trade policy choices and their implementation. The WTO's Trade Policy Review Mechanism is supposed to do just that. But it hardly makes a difference, stuck in the far-away bureaucratic straightjacket of Geneva. Ultimately, there is no substitute for independent, in-country "transparency boards" on trade policy. These could be statutory public bodies, or independent think-tanks, or a mix of the two. Uniquely, Australia has a statutory transparency board in the form of the Productivity Commission. The latter, when it was called the Tariff Board and later the Industries Assistance Commission, played an instrumental role in exposing the costs of Australian protectionism and paved the way for the opening of the economy in the 1980s.

Political constraints probably militate against transparency boards with real teeth within most, maybe all, ASEAN countries. But would an embryonic ASEAN Transparency Board, focusing on cross-border trade and FDI measures in the region, and with modest beginnings, be possible? Giving real life to the ASEAN Trade Repository as well as to the already planned ASEAN implementation scorecard would be the right places to start. But the resulting information and analysis must be available to the public, and business constituencies must be encouraged to plug in, if these ideas are to work. It would be no use to smother such mechanisms within the safe bounds of ASEAN inter-governmentalism, cut off from business and the public.

CONCLUSION

To get real: ASEAN collectively will only work bottom-up if policies and institutions improve in its individual members, particularly the leading ones. I do not foresee a realistic alternative to renewed unilateral liberalization of trade and FDI, with accompanying competitive emulation, to accelerate regional and global economic integration. That is the key to extending MNE supply chains in the region, spreading wider across manufacturing and into parts of services and agriculture, and even opening up regional markets for domestic producers and consumers. The WTO is not going to deliver much, if any, liberalization in the Doha Round or after it. Nor are FTAs. Probably the same holds true for ASEAN as well as ASEAN-plus initiatives (such as ASEAN+3 and ASEAN+6). The challenge is to get country-by-country autonomous liberalization revved up again in Southeast Asia, this time going beyond border barriers to tackle non-border regulatory barriers. That is indeed a steep hill to climb, but one that is more scaleable than top-down liberalization through trade negotiations and international and regional institutions.

ASEAN can be useful at the margin. It can be a chat forum, cement unilateral liberalization and help to prevent its reversal in difficult times, and gradually improve mutual surveillance and transparency. In short, in the regional economic context, it could be a mix of the G-20, WTO and OECD.

I view ASEAN the same way as international institutions such as the WTO, IMF, World Bank, and the new kid on the block, the G-20. I view them as a realist, a pragmatic, empirical Anglo-Saxon and Asian. Such organizations can be of value at the margin, but only with realistic goals and instruments. I do not view them through a Cartesian, French-style or Brussels-style lens. They are not, nor should they be, grand designs with grand ambitions. That is silly "global-governance" chatter, oblivious to the real-world limits to international collective action. Going down this route is more than a needless distraction; it is a recipe for misguided policies, bureaucratic mess and all-round stalemate in trying to achieve the impossible.

I would apply the same lessons to ASEAN. A cynical view holds that "The ASEAN Way" subsumes lofty rhetoric, ambitions, visions and blueprints, all convenient window-dressing to cover inter-governmental cracks and present the appearance of harmony — while governments get on separately with their national agendas. That would be a hyper-cynical reading of the ASEAN Charter. To the hard-boiled realist, such an ASEAN Way has its merits. But, if taken to extremes, it makes ASEAN a mere rhetorical exercise. It could be more than that — providing policy-makers and opinion-formers lower their ambitions and expectations and ground them in *terra firma*.

SUMMARY OF KEY POINTS

S. Tiwari

Looking at the "new-look ASEAN", the author as a "sceptical outsider", wonders whether there would be a true ASEAN Economic Community — an integrated market for goods, services, investment and skilled labour — by 2015. That is because ASEAN had no "single market" in the European sense or even in the North American sense (that is, regional production for regional consumption). It is also way off-track to talk of emulating the European Union model in terms of building common institutions and strengthening common policies. The European Union model is not relevant to ASEAN. Political, economic, cultural and institutional gaps in Southeast Asia are historically larger than they are in Europe; and there is very little common tradition, cultural or otherwise, to draw on for anything more than a very shallow integration.

What regional integration existed in ASEAN is the product of unilateral measures by individual ASEAN countries, progressively emulated by other ASEAN countries. Such unilateral liberalization of trade and foreign direct investment (FDI) had itself been partial and patchy, mainly bunched in manufacturing sectors and more limited in agriculture and services, which explains the lack of regional integration in these sectors.

On the ATIGA, it is doubted whether ASEAN's existing deadlines to eliminate non-tariff barriers (NTBs) would be met. However, the ATIGA's call for the establishment of an ASEAN Trade Repository (ATR) is praised as a good idea.

The author sees the ACIA as beneficial. The potential advantages of the ACIA are: the extension of national treatment to ASEAN-based foreign investors from the start; the wider scope of investments covered; a single negative list for scheduling reservations; and a new investor-to-state dispute settlement mechanism to complement existing ASEAN state-to-state dispute settlement. Potentially, these improvements could strengthen investment liberalization and investor protection.

8

IMPLICATIONS OF AN UNCERTAIN GLOBAL ECONOMY ON INTEGRATION INITIATIVES

Eduardo Pedrosa

In 2003 the Association of Southeast Asian Nations (ASEAN) agreed to establish an Economic Community (AEC) which would transform the region into a single market and production base which would make the region a more dynamic and stronger segment of the global supply chain. This plan was given further form in 2007 by the adoption of the ASEAN Economic Community Blueprint. The ASEAN Trade in Goods Agreement (ATIGA) and ASEAN Comprehensive Investment Agreement (ACIA) are intended to turn the vision of a single market into a reality.

However, these plans come at time of unprecedented uncertainty in the global economy. This chapter will address the implications of the crisis for the region's plans, how ATIGA and ACIA are different from previous agreements, and what else the region might add to its agenda to increase its competitiveness.

CRISIS CHANGING DRIVERS OF GROWTH

Analysis of a survey conducted by the Pacific Economic Cooperation Council (PECC) in May, showed that Southeast Asians believed that while the global economic outlook was dim, especially for the United States, Japan, and Southeast Asia, it was less so for emerging giants, China and India. The implication of this is that there is at least a perception that the traditional final markets for ASEAN's production — Western industrialized economies — are unlikely to be as robust a source of demand as in the past — but hopes remain for demand for these emerging giants.

IS THE GROWTH MODEL SHIFTING?

The same PECC survey indicates an expectation that the crisis will accelerate the regional economic integration process, especially among Southeast Asian respondents. Furthermore, a large majority of 76 per cent of Southeast Asian respondents agreed that "*slower growth in Western industrialized countries for the foreseeable future will encourage a shift to domestic demand growth in Asian economies*". This change in global demand structure has profound implications for ASEAN's plans. The critical question is whether the AEC Blueprint and its implementing agreements such as ATIGA and ACIA are predicated on a pre-crisis understanding of the global economy.

OLD WINE IN NEW BOTTLES?

The ATIGA and ACIA both contain many of the same provisions from previous ASEAN economic agreements. However, they do go beyond them in some key aspects. The creation of an ASEAN Trade Repository where tariff and non-tariff measures applied to a good are listed is a major step towards making the regional trading regime more transparent. Another plus is that the liberalization of the investment regime will be applied to both ASEAN and ASEAN-based investors. However, again, because of the changes taking place in the global economy, it is far from clear whether the ATIGA and ACIA alone are enough to increase the region's competitiveness. It may be less a case of old wine in new bottles than the wrong prescription.

An earlier survey by PECC showed that the major impediments to economic integration from a Southeast Asian perspective are not the border measures like tariffs or even rules-of-origin, but domestic, behind the border constraints especially infrastructure (see Figure 8.1). This points to a different kind of agenda that ASEAN could be adopting to enhance its competitiveness. If businesses are to use the region as a single production base then they need to accompanied by significant domestic structural reform.

It should come as little surprise that the lack of infrastructure is the top barrier to integration in the region; over 75 per cent of respondents to the survey cited infrastructure as a serious to very serious barrier. In this regard, there is little ASEAN as an organization can do per se. It is not a development agency and therefore there should not be an expectation that ASEAN can solve this problem. However, where ASEAN and its plan for an economic community can make an impact is the creation of an environment where investors — domestic and foreign — have the confidence to invest in major projects. The ACIA provides a framework for this, but success is contingent on low levels of reservations and domestic implementation.

The emphasis that PECC's opinion-leaders' survey places on behind-the-border issues is borne out by the World Bank's *Ease of Doing Business* indicators. The cost of exporting a container from ASEAN members, with the exception of Malaysia and Singapore, is significantly higher than that of sending from China. The cost of sending a container from China is US$460, while sending from Indonesia is US$704, the Philippines US$810, and land-locked Laos

FIGURE 8.1

Barriers to Economic Integration

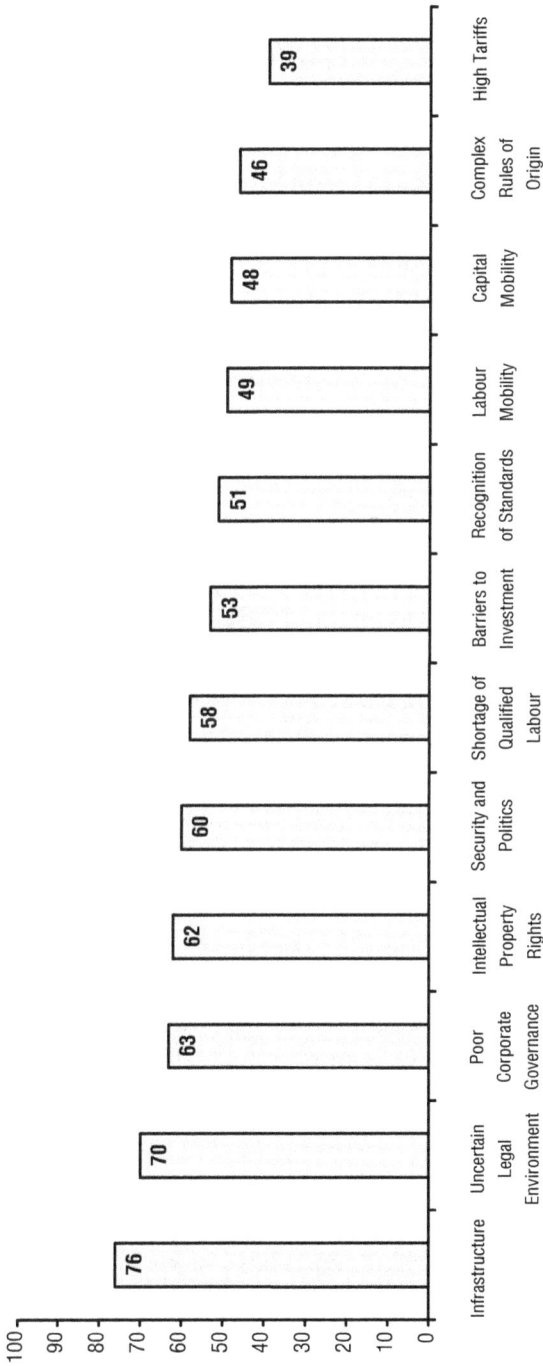

Source: PECC State of the Region 2008.

US$1,930 (see Figure 8.2). This high cost of transportation is especially important for archipelagic Southeast Asian and its ability to compete for business effectively.

Since the Asian financial crisis, the region has seen a worrying drop in foreign direct investment. The intention of the ACIA is to bring back investors by creating a free and open investment regime based on international best practices. It is supposed to facilitate the transformation of ASEAN into an investment hub that would be able to compete effectively with other emerging economies. In addition to providing protection for investors it also grants immediate benefits to ASEAN investors and ASEAN-based foreign investors, with the deadline to achieve free and open investment shortened to 2015.

This is a welcome development as the differentiation of incentives for ASEAN and non-ASEAN investors had been contradictory to the aim of gaining foreign investment for the region. Moreover, substantial work has been done to bring the agreement in line with best practices of other international agreements including the NAFTA, U.S. Model Investment Text, and the OECD Guidelines for Multinational Enterprises.

The challenge will be in implementation. The problem is not so much in the regional framework but in the environment that prevails within each individual member state. Again, according to the World Bank's *Ease of Doing Business* indicators, ASEAN member states are too slow in enforcing contracts. While China takes 406 days to enforce a contract, Thailand takes 479 days, Indonesia 570 days and the Philippines 842 days. Given the lack of capacity of the region's legal systems to deal with contract enforcement issues, investors will remain wary of investing in a region where many judicial systems remain at best slow and at worst opaque if not corrupt — in spite of any potential benefits that come from the ASEAN integration process. This correlates very closely with the second highest barrier to integration cited in the PECC survey — the uncertain legal environment.

FIGURE 8.2
Cost to Trade: US$ per Container

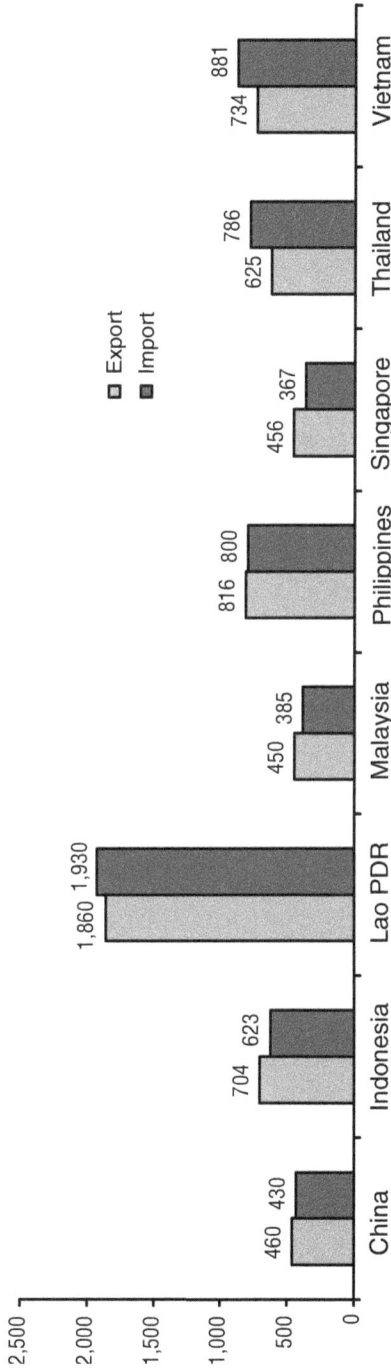

	Export	Import
China	460	430
Indonesia	704	623
Lao PDR	1,860	1,930
Malaysia	450	385
Philippines	816	800
Singapore	456	367
Thailand	786	625
Vietnam	881	734

Source: World Bank, *Ease of Doing Business 2009.*

FIGURE 8.3
Enforcing Contracts: Days to Settle

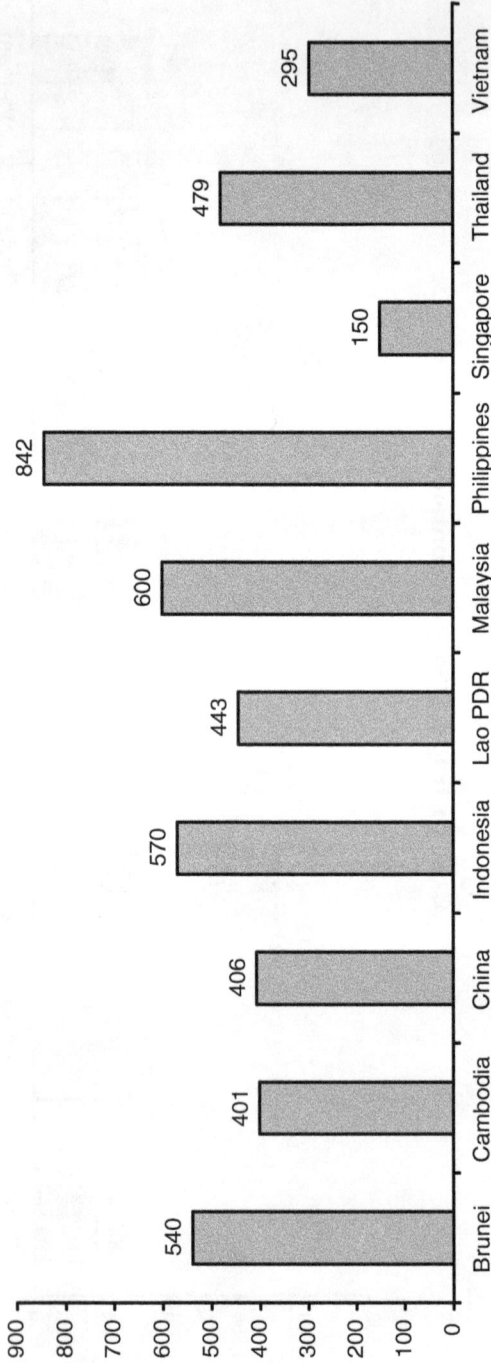

Source: World Bank, *Ease of Doing Business 2009.*

Moreover, the ACIA is a work-in-progress, with the details of what each individual member will do to be announced. There remains the potential for substantial reservation lists which could further impede the process of integration rather than accelerating it. ASEAN members need to prioritize the integration process and coordinate their reservation lists if businesses are to make the ACIA.

IMPLEMENTATION AND ENGAGEMENT

Previous ASEAN economic agreements have in the past received criticisms for being "paper agreements". Does the ASEAN Charter give hope that these agreements will be different? The Charter itself leaves dispute settlement in the hands of existing mechanisms specific to individual agreements. However, there are two developments that may prove that this time is different: the AEC Scorecard and the ASEAN Trade Repository.

The ASEAN Economic Community Scorecard could be a very useful monitoring tool to put pressure on members to live up to their commitments made through the ATIGA and ACIA. In the absence of a supranational enforcement mechanism, the publication of the Scorecard would at least enable a transparent assessment process — naming and shaming.

The ASEAN Trade Repository is intended to serve as a single reference point for all tariff and non-tariff measures applied to goods entering, exiting and transiting a country, including all governmental requirements (documentation and procedures) regarding a specific commodity. The ATR could be an extremely useful tool for the AEC. For businesses, especially small and medium enterprises it provides an easy way to gauge the costs of entering a market. Most of all, the ATR promises to provide a unique tool for transparency, perhaps more so than the Scorecard, of the process individual economies are making to achieve their goal of a single market.

AN ADDITIONAL AGENDA: STRUCTURAL REFORM

Even if ASEAN members do implement these plans, the changes in the global economy taking place because of the crisis mean that additional efforts are needed if the region is to return to anything like the rates of growth seen in earlier decades. These are the behind-the-border issues that only genuine structural reform can address. The Asia Pacific Economic Cooperation (APEC) forum has had for a few years a dialogue on structural reform, benefiting from its broader membership of both developed and developing economies. ASEAN could tap into the APEC process and see what an ASEAN structural reform agenda might look like.

TOWARDS A RULES-BASED ASEAN?

In conclusion, one way of interpreting the adoption of the ASEAN Charter is that it will turn ASEAN into more of a rules-based organization. Several important steps need to be taken to make the Charter a reality for ASEAN's peoples, there are questions of enabling legislation even though the Charter has been ratified by all members. However, through its very existence the Charter has an important symbolic value. It has created an expectation that things will change. This expectation puts pressure on members to live up to their commitments. The implementation of the ATIGA and ACIA will be important tests on whether the ASEAN Charter has changed anything or if these remain action plans with an emphasis on plans rather than action.

Note

The views expressed here are the author's own and not necessarily those of the PECC nor its constituent members.

SUMMARY OF KEY POINTS

S. Tiwari

(a) Implications of Crisis on ASEAN's Plans

The ATIGA and ACIA are intended to turn the ASEAN vision of a single market into reality. However these plans have come at a time of unprecedented uncertainty in the global economy. This chapter discusses the implications of the crisis for the region's plans and what else the region might add to its agenda to increase its competitiveness.

(b) Crisis Changing Drivers of Growth

The results of a survey carried out in May 2009 by the Pacific Economic Cooperation Council (PECC) showed that Southeast Asians believed that while the global economic outlook was dim, it was less so for the emerging giants, China and India. There was a perception that while the traditional final markets for ASEAN's production — Western industrialized economies — were unlikely to be as robust a source of demand as in the past, hopes remained for demand from the emerging giants.

(c) Possible Shifting of the Growth Model

The same survey indicated an expectation, especially among Southeast Asian respondents, that the crisis would accelerate the regional economic integration process. Of these, 76 per cent felt that "slower growth in Western industrialized countries for the foreseeable future will encourage a shift to domestic demand growth in Asian economies". This change in the global demand structure has profound implications for ASEAN's plans. The critical question thus is whether the ASEAN Economic Community Blueprint and its implementing agreements such as ATIGA and ACIA are predicated on a pre-crisis understanding of the global economy.

(d) Scorecard

The ASEAN Economic Community Scorecard is a useful monitoring tool to put pressure on ASEAN members to live up to their commitments made through the ATIGA and ACIA. The publication of the Scorecard would at least enable a transparent assessment process — naming and shaming.

(e) ATR — A Cost Gauge and Transparency Tool?

The ATR could be an extremely useful tool for the AEC. It provides an easy way for businesses — especially small and medium enterprises — to gauge the costs of entering a market. Further, it is an unique tool for transparency, perhaps more so than the scorecard, of the progress individual economies are making to achieve their goal of a single market.

9

CHALLENGES TO ACHIEVING THE ASEAN ECONOMIC COMMUNITY

David Parsons

ATIGA AND ACIA — IMPORTANT DEVELOPMENTS FOR BUSINESS

The ATIGA and ACIA are important developments in ASEAN for the business community:

- They consolidate many existing agreements thereby providing more coherence and transparency for business;
- They have been improved and modernized to address the complex linkages needed for doing business in an integrated market; and
- They provide more policy certainty for business by fleshing out how ASEAN intends to build its single market.

THE INFORMATION CHALLENGE

Even though they are not entirely new, the agreements contain a huge amount of information of policy significance to business and it will not be easy for business to absorb this information and assess the new opportunities that can emerge.

It is vital that ASEAN governments, the ASEAN Secretariat and the business community address the information gap very quickly. The gap needs to be filled through better access to information, information that can be understood by business, and socialization of that information.

Some ASEAN countries have built websites specifically for business and they are very helpful. However, not all developing countries in ASEAN have the capacity to duplicate these types of websites and that may not be an effective use of resources for much of the information about ASEAN. Rather, the ASEAN Secretariat should be the information hub of the emerging economic community. It should be provided with sufficient funds and resources to build a single business Web portal that can be supplemented by government and business in individual countries.

ASEAN documents must be translated into a language and format that is useful and practical for business, especially for smaller and medium sized firms who may not be as familiar with analysing formal international agreements.

At present, it is difficult to design socialization programmes for business with information in the current format. And with only six years to go before the AEC is to go into full effect, there is an urgent need for more socialization for business in ASEAN on a significant scale.

The goal is to enable business to become the principal actor in shaping the ASEAN Economic Community. It is not just a matter of a campaign about the benefits of agreements. The business community must be able to develop the knowledge and capacity to act on the market signals inherent in these agreements.

THE IMPLEMENTATION CHALLENGE

Implementation is probably the biggest challenge and one in which ASEAN and its governments will have to earn their credibility with business.

There is a perception that implementation schedules in ASEAN can be allowed to slip without very serious implications and that ASEAN governments are too polite to deal very earnestly with each other on implementation issues.

Unfortunately, these signals are very readily picked up by business. In order to shape the AEC in the coming years, it will be important for ASEAN and its governments to develop a real capacity to influence business expectations about the future. For this to happen, business needs to believe firmly that a future policy action really will take place as scheduled.

ASEAN has developed its scorecard for the AEC implementation schedule, which itself is an expansive document. The ASEAN Secretariat is responsible for conducting the scoring process and it will be in the form of a matrix. However, it appears that the full scoring matrix may not be a very effective instrument and will not be available to the public.

This is very unfortunate and reveals a lack of understanding of how important it is to give all businesses, including foreign investors, full assurances about the commitment of ASEAN governments in implementation and full explanations if implementation schedules cannot be met.

It should be remembered that the quality of the implementation process can be as important as checking the boxes in the scorecard matrix. Business is interested in the "market value" of implementation. In this respect, the timing and sequencing of implementation is one area that governments should continue to focus on.

In the end, business will implicitly or explicitly do its own evaluation of the implementation process and this will be reflected in the growth of investment.

There is value in the idea raised at a previous ISEAS/ASEAN Studies Centre Workshop of establishing an independent evaluation process of AEC implementation in the context of business interests.

At the time the issue was raised, it was suggested that business could do this in cooperation with analytical units such as the ASEAN

Studies Centre or set up an associated ASEAN Business Policy Centre which would not only evaluate implementation but look more comprehensively at business interests in ASEAN.

THE COMPETITION CHALLENGE WITHIN ASEAN

ASEAN's goal with the AEC is to gain a larger share of global investment and trade. Individual ASEAN countries must compete within that context to increase or at last maintain their current shares of that trade and investment growth.

If they cannot do that, the single market in production and consumption is not really in their interest. This is a concern for business in countries like Indonesia which have a large domestic market. If, for example, trade liberalization runs too far ahead of investment liberalization, there is an incentive for investors to establish their businesses in other parts of the market.

This is an area for all ASEAN countries to watch when they consider the reservations or exceptions lists in trade or investment.

It is especially important to consider all aspects of an integrated supply chain. For example, a foreign investor wanting to invest in a particular manufacturing sector may want to take a stake in several aspects of the production chain in one ASEAN country in order to make that investment viable and secure. However, if one part of the chain is not yet sufficiently open for foreign investment in that country, the whole investment could be jeopardized.

This issue could become more acute in the process of specialization which is likely to happen much more in a single market such as ASEAN where comparative advantage will be increasingly determined in sub-sectors.

SUMMARY OF KEY POINTS

S. Tiwari

The ATIGA and ACIA have provided more coherence and transparency, improved and modernized the complex linkages needed for doing business in an integrated market, and provided more policy certainty for businesses by fleshing out how ASEAN intended to build its single market.

Some challenges to achieving the AEC are:

(a) Addressing the Information Gap

It is not easy for businesses to absorb the huge amount of information in the ATIGA and ACIA that have policy significance for business and assess the new opportunities that could emerge. A joint effort by ASEAN governments, the ASEAN Secretariat and the business community to address the information gap is needed. The ASEAN Secretariat should take the lead in this with a user-friendly business Web portal that could be supplemented by government and business in individual countries.

(b) The Quality of Implementation

ASEAN has developed a scorecard for the AEC implementation schedule. It is important that the scoring matrix be available to the public. Businesses are interested in the "market value" of implementation and would implicitly or explicitly do their own evaluation of the implementation process. This would be reflected in the growth of investment. The quality of the implementation process could be as important.

(c) How ASEAN Countries Should Compete

ASEAN's goal with regard to the AEC is to gain a larger share of global investment and trade. Individual ASEAN countries must compete within that context to increase or at least maintain their current share of trade and investment growth. Accordingly, ASEAN countries need to be careful when they consider their reservations or exceptions lists in trade or investment. If, for example, trade liberalization runs too far ahead of investment liberalization, there is incentive for investors to establish their businesses in other parts of the market.

10

ASEAN
An Integrated Market?

Martin Hutagalung

The ASEAN Trade in Goods Agreement (ATIGA) and the ASEAN Comprehensive Investment Agreement (ACIA) are both world-class agreements. They are comprehensive and include key principles in international trade, such as the free transfer of capital; full protection and security for investments; fair and equitable treatment for investors; dispute resolution; and others. However, the agreements will only realize their great potential for ASEAN and the ASEAN Economic Community (AEC) if their implementation is just as comprehensive.

The timely and consistent implementation of both agreements will bring huge benefits for ASEAN as it will make the region a more attractive investment destination. The implementation of the ATIGA, ACIA as well as the realization of the AEC by 2015 would lead to significantly increased investment into the ASEAN region.

At the moment however, most senior business executives with knowledge of the region will tell you that they do not perceive ASEAN as an integrated and cohesive market. They still tend to see ASEAN as ten different markets with ten different rules and regulations. They see ASEAN as ten smaller economies instead of one market of 600 million people, with a US$1 trillion GDP and total trade of about US$1.4 trillion. So although they would like to develop an "ASEAN strategy" to take advantage of economies of scale, in reality, they can only adopt strategies for individual member countries.

The challenge for ASEAN is to convince the private sector that ASEAN is serious about realizing the AEC by 2015 and that it will implement the various agreements and roadmaps it has put in place without further delay and without backtracking on commitments it has made.

It is recommended that the ASEAN Secretariat be more proactive in informing the private sector about initiatives under the AEC, the ASEAN Charter, ATIGA/ACIA and other agreements that would benefit businesses with operations in ASEAN. The ASEAN Secretariat Website should be fully utilized to inform the private sector of what ASEAN and the ASEAN Secretariat are doing to push for greater integration. In addition, the ASEAN Secretariat could benefit greatly from transforming its website into a clearinghouse for information, such as customs information. This could also significantly improve transparency, and will help companies take advantage of existing trade benefits.

As ASEAN pushes towards greater integration, companies will increasingly require a straightforward regulatory system for their ASEAN-wide business strategies to work. As a start, all ASEAN member countries are encouraged to publish all of their laws and regulations which pertain to economic matters. Ideally, a webpage containing a list of all common regulations would be generated, with links to each individual countries' rules displayed on the same website.

There should also be more consultation with the private sector. ASEAN is to be commended for recognizing the business community as an important stakeholder in the future of the AEC. To formalize private sector consultation further, it is hoped that ASEAN will introduce a "notice and comment" mechanism, where members of both the private and public sectors can discuss necessary change. It is also hoped that member countries will recognize the value of incorporating private sector input into the formulation of laws affecting business and industry. Private sector should not only be seen as a source for feedback but also as project partners providing resources and expertise.

In conclusion, ASEAN is commended for the ASEAN Trade in Goods Agreement and the ASEAN Comprehensive Investment Agreement. The U.S.-ASEAN Business Council fully supports initiatives that will bring about a more integrated ASEAN and create more certainty in doing business in the region. When ASEAN is fully integrated, multinational companies can view ASEAN as one region, rather than a collection of individual countries.

SUMMARY OF KEY POINTS

S. Tiwari

This chapter provides the perspective of U.S. businesses in ASEAN.

The challenge for ASEAN is to convince the private sector that ASEAN is serious about realizing the AEC by 2015 and that it would implement the agreements and roadmaps it has put in place without further delay and without backtracking on commitments made.

Most senior business executives with knowledge of the region do not perceive ASEAN as an integrated and cohesive market, but as ten different markets with ten different sets of rules and regulations. They see ASEAN as ten smaller economies instead of one market of 600 million people, with a US$1 trillion GDP and total trade of about US$1.4 trillion.

Although they would like to develop an "ASEAN strategy" to take advantage of economies of scale, in reality, they can only adopt strategies for individual member countries.

The author offered two other suggestions to take ASEAN forward:

(i)   The ASEAN Secretariat should be more proactive in informing the private sector about initiatives under the AEC, the ASEAN Charter, the ATIGA, the ACIA and other agreements that would benefit businesses with operations in ASEAN.

(ii) As ASEAN pushes towards greater integration, companies would increasingly require a straightforward regulatory system for their ASEAN-wide business strategies to work. As a start, all ASEAN member countries are encouraged to publish their laws and regulations pertaining to economic matters. Ideally, a webpage containing a list of all the common laws should be available, with links to each individual countries' rules displayed on the same website.

11

A MISCELLANY OF TRADE ISSUES

S. Tiwari

The business-sector presentations were followed by views expressed by business personalities, ASEAN officials and those from think-tanks specializing in ASEAN issues.

NON-TARIFF BARRIERS (NTBS)

It was agreed that the deadline of five years for the removal of non-tariff barriers in ATIGA was "unrealistic". It was "more of a paper assessment" but had to be retained in ATIGA as a commitment. NTBs were a "moving target" and therefore had to be eliminated on a continuous basis. It was generally felt that some non-tariff measures were necessary and accordingly it was best to adopt a "measured approach" and target "barrier components" of these measures for elimination. ASEAN planned to issue guidelines on how to implement non-tariff measures such as import licensing procedures.

ATIGA sought to eliminate NTBs through trade facilitation. Measures such as the harmonized tariff nomenclatures, the ASEAN single window, et cetera, were attempts towards making progress although they were not fully operational yet.

THE RESPONSIBILITY OF THE PRIVATE SECTOR

ASEAN Secretariat officials felt that the private sector needed to take a keener interest in ASEAN. It needed to keep abreast of ASEAN developments and "prod" the public sector.

ASEAN was considering the possibility of obtaining private-sector inputs on NTBs through a joint consultative committee on trade facilitation. It was hoped that the private sector would speak up. It was mentioned that the private sector's common excuse was that they had the "right to remain silent".

THE ISSUE OF CORRUPTION

A participant observed that the likely reason for the business people's reluctance to voice concerns was that they were "scared of retaliation" from certain authorities. He added that no one had raised the issue of corruption as a non-tariff barrier. One of the private-sector commentators felt that the silence on corruption was a manifestation of the ASEAN tendency to "keep things comfortable". He added that a survey of ASEAN businesses, across all sectors, had been carried out to determine their concerns and their perceptions in relation to non-tariff measures. However, this study had never been released, since it highlighted the issue of corruption in ASEAN.

THE SCORECARD DEMYSTIFIED

It was explained that the scorecard was specific to each ASEAN member country and tracked its "achievements", with scores given according to the percentage achieved of the total measures. As such, the scores in the scorecards could be compared across countries. This meant that the scores would be "sensitive". Notwithstanding this, the intention was to release the completed scorecards, though the released form may differ from the actual scorecard. Individual countries could also release their own scores, if they so preferred. Doing so may "pressure" other member states to fulfil their requirements. The application of peer pressure via the scorecard mechanism was a "stick" that ASEAN member countries could wield to expedite reform.

A DIFFERING VIEW

One of the commentators disagreed that the liberalization process was happening in a "bottom-up" manner. He was of the view that national governments liberalize trade, while businesses liberalize across the border. What happens was that a "copy-cat" mechanism would kick in and piecemeal liberalization would proceed apace. In his view, ASEAN as a collective body could not drive this process, and it had a "disconnect" with the real world of producers and consumers. He remained adamant that ASEAN's so-called successes were more akin to "paper exercises". Even the ASEAN– China Agreement on Trade in Goods had changed little on the ground. This was because the bulk of tariffs had already been lifted by then.

On non-tariff barriers, his view was that WTO disciplines for NTBs were weak and therefore could not contain their proliferation in this crisis. In ASEAN, Indonesia and Vietnam were the main culprits using non-tariff measures, such as import licences and public procurement, to engage in protectionism. In contrast, there has been little evidence of explicit tariff imposition as a result of the crisis. He added that he did not see Southeast Asia having a "V-shaped recovery". This was because the region was dependent on supply chains that were linked to final markets in the West, where demand was currently low. He did not see a return of demand in the West to 2007 levels. Other sources of demand had to be created, and this required "deep structural reform" in the medium term.

The commentator accepted that ASEAN had not actually compared itself to the EU model or wanted to adopt the EU model. It was the EU itself which was keen to export its model to other regions and saw ASEAN as a ready recipient.

THE WEBSITE ISSUE

On the ASEAN Website issue, it was explained that money had been spent to improve it and increase its capacity. It was agreed, however, that the ASEAN Secretariat had not yet been able to recruit the right person to manage it. It had turned out to be highly demanding and technical and the Secretariat could not afford to pay for the expertise.

12

POLICY ISSUES FOR ASEAN COUNTRIES

S. Tiwari

The conclusions and policy issues set out below arise from the presentations and discussions on the topics of the workshop's three sessions. They are set out here for consideration by ASEAN policy-makers and officials, with the hope that they will help to improve the implementation and utilization of the Charter, the ATIGA, the ACIA and the ASEAN economic integration process.

HOW TO UTILIZE ASEAN'S LEGAL PERSONALITY?

ASEAN needs to work on and settle the question of how it wishes to utilize its legal personality. This will allow the legal personality to be used meaningfully.

NEED TO MONITOR IMPLEMENTATION OF CHARTER AND ASEAN TREATIES

Article 5(2) of the Charter requires that ASEAN countries "take all necessary measures, including the enactment of appropriate domestic legislation, to effectively implement the provisions of the Charter and to comply with all obligations of membership". The domestic implementation of the ASEAN Charter will continue to occupy ASEAN for some time. Since more obligations will be created as ASEAN takes further steps to integrate its member states, it would be useful if ASEAN instituted regular monitoring and reporting processes. This would reduce bottlenecks in the implementation of the Charter and ASEAN treaties.

AN EXPECTATION OF CHANGE

The ASEAN Charter is intended to turn ASEAN into a rules-based organization. The workshop felt that through its very existence the Charter had an important symbolic value. It had created an expectation that things would change. It was thus important for ASEAN members states to live up to their commitments. The implementation of ATIGA and ACIA would be important tests as to whether the ASEAN Charter has changed anything or if these remained as action plans with an emphasis on plans rather than action.

BARRIER TO INTEGRATION — INFRASTRUCTURE

It was revealed during the workshop that according to a PECC survey, the major impediments to economic integration from a Southeast Asian perspective were the domestic, behind-the-border constraints, especially infrastructure. Over 75 per cent of respondents to the survey cited infrastructure as a "serious" to "very serious" barrier. ASEAN countries can help themselves by improving their infrastructure. They could also benefit from creating an environment where investors — domestic and foreign — have the confidence to invest in major projects.

BARRIER TO INTEGRATION — THE UNCERTAIN LEGAL ENVIRONMENT

In the light of the World Bank's Ease of Doing Business 2009 indicators and the barriers to ASEAN integration cited in the PECC survey, the workshop identified one challenge to integration as the uncertain legal environment that prevailed within each member state. For example, according to the World Bank's Ease of Doing Business indicators, ASEAN member states were slow in enforcing contracts. While China takes 406 days to enforce a contract, Thailand takes 479 days, Indonesia 570 days and the Philippines 842 days. Given the lack of capacity of the region's legal systems to deal with contract enforcement issues, it was felt that investors would remain wary of investing in a region where judicial systems — except for a few — remained at best slow and at worst opaque, in spite of any potential benefits that might accrue from the ASEAN integration process. ASEAN countries need to take action individually to correct this situation.

BUSINESSES NEED TO BELIEVE

ASEAN also needs to address a serious perception problem, the perception that implementation schedules in ASEAN could be allowed to slip without very serious implications. These signals are very readily picked up by businesses. With the impression in the business community that only 30 per cent of ASEAN agreements had been implemented, the business community and observers remained sceptical about ASEAN's will to abide by its agreements.

In order to shape the AEC in the coming years, it will be important for ASEAN and its governments to make concerted efforts to influence business expectations about the future. For this to occur, business needs to believe that a future policy action will really take place as scheduled.

THE TRADE INSTRUMENTS:
ASEAN NEEDS TO DO MORE

The workshop felt that ASEAN had moved forward through its review, rationalization, enhancement and consolidation exercises, which had produced ATIGA 2009 and ACIA 2009. It was of the view, however, that ASEAN had to do more, including:

* Working on the real obstacles to integration, which include tackling non-tariff barriers at and behind the borders;
* Tackling the regulation barriers behind the borders so as to make real progress on market access; and
* Handling the listing of reservations under ACIA 2009 in a manner ensuring that ASEAN would be an attractive investor destination.

AVOIDING IMPEDING THE INTEGRATION PROCESS

Parts of the ACIA are a work-in-progress. For example, there remains the potential for substantial reservation lists which could further impede the process of integration rather than accelerate it. It would thus be necessary for ASEAN members to prioritize the integration process and coordinate their reservation lists if businesses were to benefit from the ACIA.

A STRUCTURAL REFORM AGENDA

The changes in the global economy brought by the financial crisis meant that additional efforts are needed if the ASEAN region is to return to the kind of rates of growth seen in earlier decades. These would require ASEAN to address the behind-the-border issues that only genuine structural reform can address. The Asia Pacific Economic Cooperation (APEC) forum had for a few years a dialogue on structural reform, benefiting from the membership of both developed and developing economies. ASEAN could tap into the APEC process and see what an ASEAN structural reform agenda might look like.

NEED FOR TRANSPARENCY

Some workshop participants felt that ASEAN lacked publicly available information on many trade and investment regulations, especially of the non-tariff, behind-the-border variety. Also lacking was systematic assessment of the costs and benefits of different policies and communication of findings to the public. More transparency in all these respects would facilitate informed discussion about trade policy choices and their implementation. A suggestion was made regarding independent, in-country "transparency boards" on trade policy. These could be statutory public bodies, independent think-tanks, or a mix of the two.

The workshop was of the view that the ASEAN Trade Repository envisaged in ATIGA 2009 was a good idea, containing trade and customs laws and procedures and a variety of trade-related information. The mechanism would increase transparency. ASEAN might find it useful to study the model of the Australian Tariff Board (now called the Productivity Commission). It could be useful as a tool to create in-country independent transparency boards, leading to an ASEAN Economic Transparency Board.

THE INFORMATION CHALLENGE

The goal of ASEAN is to enable businesses to become the principal actors in shaping the AEC. The business community must thus be able to develop the knowledge and capacity to act on the market signals inherent in the ATIGA and ACIA. However, it was felt that it was not easy for businesses to absorb the huge amount of information of policy significance to business and assess the new opportunities that could emerge. It was thus vital that ASEAN governments, the ASEAN Secretariat and the business community address the information gap. The gap needed to be filled through better access to information that could be understood by business. It was suggested that the ASEAN Secretariat should be the information hub of the emerging economic community. It should be provided with sufficient funds and resources to build a user-friendly business Web portal that could be supplemented by government and business in individual countries.

ENHANCE PUBLIC- PRIVATE SECTOR CONSULTATIONS

The business community was recognized as an important stakeholder in the future of the AEC. In this connection, business-sector representatives called for an increase in consultations with the private sector. A suggestion was made that a "notice and comment" mechanism be introduced in which members of both the private and public sectors could discuss necessary changes. This might help ASEAN countries to obtain private sector ideas when formulating laws affecting business and industry.

SPREADING KNOWLEDGE ABOUT ASEAN

Awareness about ASEAN in its member states is not widespread. One of the aims of the ASEAN Charter is to promote a common ASEAN identity and a sense of belonging among its peoples. With the ASEAN Charter now in place, it is now for ASEAN to ensure that knowledge about the Charter is spread among its peoples. Hence, there should be more concerted efforts at promoting awareness of what ASEAN means for the general public and the different stakeholders. This would help bridge the information gap and overcome the current disconnect between central policy-making and the realities on the ground, paving the way towards greater transparency and accountability under the aegis of a strong and dynamic ASEAN Charter.

INDEX

www.ingramcontent.com/pod-product-compliance
Lightning Source LLC
Chambersburg PA
CBHW021540260326
41914CB00001B/93